Grow by Focusing on What Matters

Grow by Focusing on What Matters

Competitive Strategy in 3 Circles

3-circle growth™

Joel E. Urbany and James H. Davis

First published in 2010 by Joel E. Urbany and James H. Davis
Business Expert Press, LLC
222 East 46th Street, New York, NY 10017
www.businessexpertpress.com

ISBN-13: 978-1-60649-092-1 (paperback)
ISBN-10: 1-60649-092-3 (paperback)

ISBN-13: 978-1-60649-093-8 (e-book)
ISBN-10: 1-60649-073-7 (e-book)

DOI 10.4128/9781606490938

A publication in the Business Expert Press Strategic Management
collection

Collection ISSN: 2150-9611 (print)
Collection ISSN: 2150-9646 (electronic)

Cover design by Jonathan Pennell
Interior design by Scribe Inc.

First edition: December 2010

10 9 8 7 6 5 4 3 2 1

Printed in the United States of America.

Abstract

Growth and competitive advantage are about effective positioning. Building effective positioning is challenging today for firms facing new and stronger competition, volatile and uncertain markets, and shifting customer desires and demands. The 3-Circle model facilitates speed of understanding and action by focusing attention on the most critical strategy concepts in this uncertain environment. Growth strategy emerges in the model from systematically addressing four key strategy directives in a deep and disciplined way:

1. *define*, *build*, and *defend* the unique value you create for customers;
2. *correct*, *eliminate*, or *reveal* value that is failing customers, which they're not aware of;
3. potentially *neutralize* the unique value created for customers by competitors;
4. *explore* and *exploit* new growth opportunities through deep understanding of customers' unmet needs.

Keywords

Growth strategy, competitive advantage, strategic positioning, customer value, competencies, revenue/profit growth, fighting commoditization

Contents

Preface

The 3-Circle model was developed over the past several years, initially in strategic planning for a university graduate program and in an executive MBA course designed to integrate the concepts of marketing and competitive strategy. Over the course of time, the 3-Circle model has been successfully used by hundreds of organizations throughout the world in establishing and growing their market positions. Many of the case examples in this book demonstrating applications of the 3-Circle model applications are from executives who have attended executive education training at the University of Notre Dame.

The development of competitive strategy is difficult because there are a lot of moving parts, as well as hundreds of frameworks, that might potentially guide the effort. Executives appreciate how the 3-Circle model simplifies the integration of customer, firm, and competitor analysis to generate growth strategies. It also provides a common language and process for understanding and explaining competitive advantage and for identifying profitable growth strategy.

We wish to thank all the executives who have been through our courses and training. They have provided test cases and important insights that have led to the continual refinement and building of the model. Some of their comments about the model appear in the quotes here in the front end of the book. We also thank our colleagues in the academic and professional community who have provided both scholarly and practical insights that have influenced the development of the model.

Notre Dame, Indiana
January 2011

Comments From Users
of the Framework

"I have used the 3-Circle Model extensively at both Rust-Oleum and Bosch. . . . There is no simpler way to cut right to the core issues of how your products are positioned to the customer and how well you are differentiated from your competitors."

Terry Horan
President, Rotary Tools
Robert Bosch Corporation

"The 3-Circle Model is to the point, creative, and fosters creative thinking and new ideas."

Nathan Olds
National Sales Manager
Honeywell Corporation

"A disciplined approach to identifying, hypothesizing, quantifying, prioritizing, evaluating, understanding, and acting on customer needs."

Chris Bardeggia
Global Director, Quality Systems
Whirlpool Corporation

"The Three Circle process really showed our weaknesses in understanding our customers and helped us to develop a strategy to attack the market and pick up new customers . . . one by the way that is working."

Mike Lenahan
CEO
Resource Recovery Corporation

"A simple and logical pathway to properly document, analyze, and test our assumptions about our customers, competitors, and ourselves."

John Brohel
Vice-President, Finance
Cadmus Communications

"What we found from an operations side was that we were completely out of line with what our customer wanted. Almost all of our top initiatives had no impact on the items that were important to them. Only by talking with the customer and preparing the 3-Circle were we able to redefine our focus."

Dan Smith
Business Unit Manager
Federal Signal/Elgin Sweeper

"A perfect tool to help us think about what we offer, what the customer wants, and what the competition offers. Determining the differences and similarities between the customer and competitions' needs respectively is a brilliant way to reevaluate our new services."

David Burda
Senior Associate
Stockamp, a Huron Group Consulting Practice

"[The 3-Circle model] forces an objective view of my capabilities and my competitors while at the same time keeps the customer's needs in view. I thought it was a great exercise to point out what can be added in value to my company in order to grow."

William Muller
Senior Engineer, Engineering & Technical Services
Michigan Gas Utilities

"The positive benefit of using this framework was a focus on where the organization needs to focus its assets. It requires you to dissect the organization and define the specific aspects that are core . . . It also exposes the opportunity and provides a clear presentation to your audience. It is a tool that I use frequently now to really understand where we can differentiate, grow and address an unmet need."

Jason Niehaus
Vice President of Operations, COO
Mercy Hospital

"[The 3-Circle framework] gave us a relatively accurate idea of where we stood and what competencies we had that we were not using. It also made us face the fact that there were areas of the business that could be eliminated."

Kyle Cusson
General Manager, Midwest
Red Hawk Security Systems, Inc., a UTC Fire and Security Company

"[The 3-Circle process] directs a team to look at the possibilities and paints a picture of the results in a way that can be easily cascaded through an organization."

Don Marquess
Vice President, Sales
Galls—An Aramark Company

"[The 3-Circle process] generated a tremendous amount of interaction, discussion, agreements/disagreements and market dynamics awareness."

Danny Dorsey
Vice President
Cummins Bridgeway

"I think the framework helps me to more effectively communicate with groups within the company to whom we develop applications for. I add more value to the company if the software we implement helps deliver services that matter."

Tom Hoban
Application Development Manager
Harbor Capital Advisors, Inc.

"I liked the simplicity and self-explanatory nature of the 3-Circle model more than any of the more widely used models."

R. Kelley Cook
Senior IT Consultant
Ajilon Consulting

"There are lots of models available—from Porter's Five Forces to McKinsey's 7 Ss and back again; yet each has its weakness . . . It often looks too 'academic' . . . [in contrast] . . . your three-circle model gets at the three most critical areas of organizational strategy."

Bob Henson
Owner
HK & Associates (Management Consulting)

"The [3-Circle] project has allowed us to dive deeper into the service offerings we currently provide and ask how we can improve the way we market and communicate to the industry. I believe this project has also spurred a new idea for our company, that being an IT Data Analytics Service that we hope to launch in 2009. We didn't realize that we had the data internally that we believe we can turn around and sell to our clients. Overall, this project was very helpful in our overall view of our company and our competition. In fact I find myself asking 3-Circle questions when making decisions both professionally and personally."

Director of Business Development
Pharmaceutical Industry

"In one exercise, the ability to articulate what the company felt was valued by the customer . . . the customer's perceptions of important attributes . . . and areas that were of potential new business growth."

Karen Kenney
Senior R&D Director
Fortune 500 Corporation

"The framework provides a relatively rapid process to hone in on sources of competitive advantage . . . helps clients understand the fundamental building blocks for effective strategy development."

Senior Consultant
Consulting Firm

CHAPTER 1

The Challenges of Growth

Sara Johnson owns a pet store. She started this small business out of a passion for helping people take care of their pets. The store is off to a good start, but she really worries about how she will grow the business. The competitive environment that surrounds her store is challenging, with the big-box stores having full-blown pet departments, specialty stores improving, and Web-based operations providing access to low-priced supplies. In addition, customer needs seem to change over time.

In contrast, Ken Smith is a brand manager for a $900 million division of a major consumer products company. Ken worries about the exact same things as Sara, just on a different scope and scale. He has customers who have supported 8% growth of his product lines in each of the last 2 years. His challenge, though, is how to maintain that growth rate (representing $72 million in sales) in markets where competitive imitation over time has led the products to become very similar and competitive advantage more difficult to come by.

The context and magnitude of these problems are quite different, but, at the root, they are the same. Whether you are Sara or Ken, the general manager of an insurance company seeking to increase policies sold, a United Way director seeking to increase donations, or a human resource director wishing to increase business with internal staff in their hiring decisions, your question is, how do we successfully position against the competition and grow our business? While a complex matter, the task of building growth strategy has some simple foundational ideas. The goal of this book is to teach these fundamental concepts to you so that you can implement them and then teach others.

The teaching requires breaking down what seems like a complex task into simpler component parts. While you will have no trouble understanding the component parts—such as customer value, competitive position differences, and firm capabilities—what most firms struggle with is how you *integrate* them in building effective growth strategy. In this chapter, we will consider the fundamentals of competitive strategy at the heart of the framework we use and the reasons why integrating these principles is difficult and rare. Yet we will also point out that businesses that practice such integration make more money. At the core of all this is the notion that you cannot grow your company (or your school, your nonprofit, your relationships, the happiness of your volunteers, for that matter) without really understanding the value your "customers" seek and the value that you can create for them.

Three Fundamentals

Having lost a teenage brother to an auto accident in his youth, CEO Peter Lewis of Progressive Insurance was driven by a deep understanding of human needs surrounding auto insurance. Further fueled by his distaste for abysmal turnaround times on claims in the industry, Lewis decided—in the face of much resistance within his company—that Progressive would become a company with the capability of providing an immediate-response claims service. Progressive's well-known growth from small niche competitor to one of the "Big 4" auto insurance firms owes everything to Peter Lewis's intuitive, tenacious application of three basic principles of positioning strategy.[1]

The first principle is defining advantage from the *perspective of customer value*.[2] Lewis saw dissatisfaction with response times where others in the industry did not. Further, he understood why it was important. Delay in claims processing causes inconvenience and adds stress to already stressful situations for drivers having had an accident who seek fast resolution and peace of mind. The second principle is developing insight about opportunity in a way that *differentiates* from the competition.[3] So while many firms in the industry would define their business purpose as "paying auto accident claims," Lewis instead described Progressive's as "reducing the human trauma and economic costs of automobile accidents." Other competitors either did not recognize the opportunity or simply accepted poor claims-adjustment service and response time because all firms were following the same antiquated model.

Just developing a positioning strategy is not enough, however. The third principle centers around developing *distinctive capabilities, resources, and assets* to execute the positioning strategy.[4] Progressive built skill in technology development, process design, and human resources. Over a period of years, the company developed proprietary software and databases, specific selection and development skills for hiring and training employees, as well as a disciplined measurement culture to manage continuous improvement.

In sum, in his search for growth, Peter Lewis intuitively and persistently followed these three fundamental principles:

- Create important value for customers
- Be different from (better than) the competition
- Build and leverage your capabilities with an eye toward the desired customer value

While almost simple enough to be intuitively obvious, it is easy to lose sight of these principles. In fact, there are a variety of forces that get in the way of their effective implementation.

Challenge 1: Limited Integration of Strategy Perspectives

It turns out that it is difficult for an individual—let alone a complex organization—to simultaneously hold the three principles of strategy in mind. Multiple goals imply multiple, often costly, efforts to achieve them. Potential conflict between, and trade-offs among, the three goals of beating the competitor, creating value for customers, and leveraging our capabilities make it natural for firms to treat them separately. Illustrative of this is a study of strategic focus in decision making, conducted by George Day and Prakash Nedungadi of the Wharton School, which found that 77% of the organizations studied had a "single-minded" focus;[5] that is, the organizations largely focused on either customers, competitors, or the internal workings of the company but rarely any of the three together. Three distinct types of firms were identified in the study: self-centered firms (i.e., focused on internal factors; 33%), customer-centered firms (31%), and competitor-centered firms (13%).

These single-minded views are suboptimal, however. Day and Nedungadi found that 16% of the firms they studied were *market driven*, that is, focused jointly on competitors and customers, and that these firms reported significantly superior financial performance relative to the other firms in the study. Similarly, other research has found that a more integrated view of company, customers, and competitors leads to greater profitability.[6] Yet the striking point is that firms that do an effective job of integrating are in the minority. The more common tendency to be single-minded limits the search for growth opportunities and may be self-perpetuating.[7]

Challenge 2: Knowing Customers

Most decisions that involve customers are made without customer research. Firms have neither the time nor the resources to devote to every customer-related decision. Interestingly, though, even when sophisticated, large-sample research is conducted for particular decisions, it may frequently fall by the wayside because the research is shouted down by managers with prior agendas that contradict research findings.

Challenge 2a: Truly Understanding Customer Values and Beliefs

Although they may at times dismiss formal research, we know that smart managers talk to customers and know them, often over many years. So it is fair to say more informal research is the norm. In this sense, it is difficult for managers to believe that they "don't know" customers. Yet there is much research that suggests the opposite. To understand why, consider a particularly telling study from University of Chicago researchers Harry Davis, Steve Hoch, and Easton Ragsdale. Davis and his colleagues asked pairs of experimental subjects to estimate each other's preferences for new product concepts. The new product concepts were a mix of higher-priced durable goods, lower-priced durables and nondurables, and services. For each concept, each subject was asked to estimate both the probability that they would purchase the concept in the future *and* the probability that the *person they were paired with* would purchase the concept. Across four studies, which varied the amount of information provided for the concepts (verbal description only vs. verbal description and pictorial representation) and the dependent measure used, the authors found the same results. Despite showing confidence in their estimates, the subjects showed substantial error in predicting their partners' preferences. Only about half of them predicted more accurately than a naïve forecast that used the average of the gender-specific preferences. The authors found a strong tendency for a person to use their own preferences for the new concept to predict the preferences of their partner.

The most remarkable thing about this research, however, is that the subject pairs were not strangers. Across all the studies, *husbands* were paired with *wives*.[8] In spite of intimate familiarity with each other, spouses demonstrated significant error in projecting each other's preferences, with error coming largely from two sources. First, the husband (or wife) tried to project their own preferences onto the other, when in fact their preference was not similar to their spouse's. Second, when the husband-wife preferences *were* similar, error was introduced when the spouse *overadjusted* for what he or she thought would be a difference in his or her mate's preference relative to their own.

This leads us to a key question: If people who live together and know each other intimately make such errors in predicting each other's preferences, how can product and marketing managers NOT be subject to the similar errors in predicting customers' values? There is a fair amount of academic research that finds significant error in managerial judgment of consumer attitudes, beliefs, and behavior.[9] Further evidence of this comes from surveys of our own executive students and clients. They predict customer beliefs with good confidence yet express significant surprise (and opportunity!) when they subsequently conduct primary research with customers.[10]

In fact, this should not be surprising. In the day-to-day operation of a business, the immediate challenges often center on internal concerns, which tend to be very concrete, top of mind, and unavoidable. Managers spend most of their time inside, managing people and resources. The capacities within the firm need to be organized, people need to be developed, budgets need to be met. There may in fact be a bias against spending time to understand the customer's perspective on our products and services because hearing bad news would mean that our products, processes, people selection and development, and execution would have to be changed, which is no easy task. Instead, it is very easy to assume "we know the customer."

Challenge 2b: Understanding Customer Evaluations of Competitors

While most companies ask customers how their company is doing, many do not seek comparative customer views of *competitors*. One firm, which we will call Food Supplier, Inc., for example, happily found—through interviews in a 3-Circle project with one customer segment (independent restaurants)—that the company was hitting on a number of important points of value for customers, many relating to delivery, warehousing, and sales support. Consistent with their expectations, this suggested that the company was providing customers a great deal of value. Yet the research also explored customer perception of *competitor* value. This produced the startling conclusion that the key competitor matched every point-of-value provided by Food Supplier, Inc., but it was also perceived as having far superior accuracy in deliveries and invoicing, as well as premium food quality at competitive prices. This analysis opened the executive team's eyes to opportunities for a new process improvement program in operations and sales to enhance competitive superiority in key functional areas, as well as a new marketing program to clearly communicate the differential customer value created by these new internal programs. Since that implementation, the company has experienced increases in same-store sales and has extended these standardized processes to other areas of the company.

Common Strategic Mistakes in Evaluating Competitive Differences

Most of us face the difficulty of integrating relevant competitive, company, and customer facts, as well as the challenge of truly knowing customers' natural biases. Some may argue that these difficulties work themselves out through learning and experience. But what seems to happen is often the opposite—these biases can lead to flawed judgment about competitive advantage. This is because we anchor our beliefs in these early observations and we are not likely to change them. In companies we work with, we see, over and over, the following three strategic errors that result from the biases discussed earlier:

1. We think we are different from competitors, but we are not really different in the customer's eyes.

2. We are different from competitors, but in ways that are not really important to customers.

3. We are different from competitors in ways that matter to customers, but we do not have the resources or capabilities to build and sustain those differences.

In fact, what is needed is a way of thinking and a process that helps us to simultaneously think about customers, competitors, and the company, and that puts our existing beliefs to the test. That is the primary goal of the 3-Circle model and the process we will teach you in this book. Let us illustrate the key concepts.

Thinking Integratively About Customer Value, Competitive Position, and Capabilities

Exploring Value

There is competitive advantage in thinking about your organization in a way that integrates the value customers seek, the value the competitor is believed to provide, and your own value-producing capabilities. A company called Ultimate Ears illustrates such thinking. A sound engineer who worked closely with big rock bands like Van Halen, Jerry Harvey was very close to the customer segment (rock musicians) and the need for sound management. The traditional technology for band members to hear their own performance was large, onstage monitors (speakers) tied to each instrument. Figure 1.1 is our first circle—the customer's circle, in this case representing the value sought by rock and roll musicians in the sound equipment used by the band to hear its own performance. Here is the key benefit that a band desires from that equipment: that it produces sound audible to the band members (seems pretty obvious!). But let us push that a little further. Why is this important to the musicians? It seems simple, but digging underneath, it is easy to see how the notion of being able to "listen to one's self play" is fundamentally related to overall performance and achievement. If the sound back to the band is audible, that enhances performance quality by allowing the band to be more precisely in sync with each other. Performance quality is fundamental to the success of the show to an audience that

Rock musicians ultimately want their sound
system (that the band hears) to contribute
to excellent show delivery.

Figure 1.1. Value sought by customers: Rock musicians and onstage sound.

is accustomed to hearing the music on precisely mixed studio record-
ings. Figure 1.2 captures the fact that the standard technology—large
onstage monitors—provides this basic quality. The circle added on the
lower left represents the customer's perception of the value provided by
the onstage monitors. As in any product or service category, there are a
number of dimensions of this value. For the moment, though, we will
focus on a few of the most important dimensions.

The overlap between the circles is strategically important. It is the
positive "equity" provided by the product in the mind of the customer—
that is, the space where value delivered meets value sought. So the onstage
monitors provide a way for the band to effectively hear the sounds of
their instruments and vocals, and positive value is produced for these
customers.

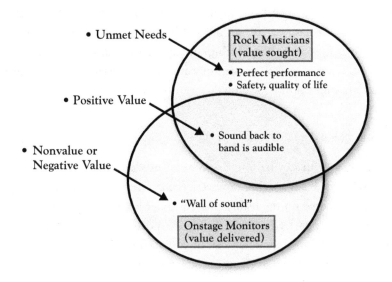

Figure 1.2. Value delivered by onstage monitors.

Nonvalue or Negative Value (Disequity)

Figure 1.2 also points out two other strategically important concepts, relating to the areas where the circles do not overlap. The nonoverlapping area to the left—which we label nonvalue or negative value (the latter also known as disequity). Many consumption experiences have nonvalue or negative value associated with them. It is the calories consumed while relishing a big hamburger, the headache after a celebratory night out, and, occasionally, it is an endemic part of a good or service that we are simply willing to put up with in the absence of a superior alternative. It is the exorbitant fees for the broker with whom you have developed a very close relationship and trust implicitly, the chatty hair stylist whose gossip you put up with because you love the way he or she cuts your hair, or the doctor you love who makes you wait forever in the waiting room. In the case of the rock musician, it is the "wall of sound" that occurs when onstage monitors are used to allow the band members to hear the instruments. This is the deafening sound onstage that escalates as each member player sequentially keeps turning up the volume on their own monitor so they can hear their instrument. That wall of sound not only gets in the way of effective performance, it has also contributed to significant hearing loss over time among rock band members.[11] For example, Alex Van Halen reports that he has lost 30% to 60% of his hearing as a result of years of sound "gas fires" occurring during onstage Van Halen shows.[12] Where a firm's products or services create nonvalue, or even negative value, there is significant opportunity for growth.

Unmet Needs

Similarly, growth can be found in unmet needs. This upper right portion of Figure 1.2 is another nonoverlapping area, critical in that it keeps attention focused on the reality that customer needs are never fully met. Musicians seek perfection in performance, possibly an ideal that cannot be achieved. Yet any edge that can be obtained to improve performance is a direct contribution to the musician's bottom line, relating to success, enjoyment, and career achievement. A second way to think more deeply about unmet needs is to ask some obvious-sounding questions about points of negative value that our product or service is creating. Why is that important enough to consumers for them to mention it? For example, one reason that the "wall of sound" problem is important to rock musicians is because it is associated with hearing loss. Why is hearing loss important? It is so obvious that we do not really think about it, yet we should think about it to understand its enormity as a consideration in decision making. As people lose their hearing, they may lose not only the capability to make a living and take care of one's family but also the ability to enjoy the people and world around them—that is, quality of later life is a deeper value that is touched by this. So how big is the value of an alternative that solves this problem? (Huge!) Would musicians be willing to pay handsomely for a superior solution? (Yes!)

Opportunity

This dilemma is where Jerry Harvey came in. Encouraged by musicians who sought something to help improve performance and to reduce hearing loss, Harvey developed the equivalent of an *in-ear* monitor, which each player on stage would have, isolating the sound of their specific instrument. This allowed the musicians to hear clearly, to know how they fit in with the other players, and to better control their own sound. These performance benefits were supplemented not only by substantial noise reduction (easier on the ears) but also by the greater room on stage given the removal of the larger onstage monitors. Figure 1.3 completes the 3-Circle picture, adding the circle on the left, which represents the value provided by Harvey's company, Ultimate Ears. The addition of the third circle creates seven distinctive areas in the Venn diagram—each labeled by a letter and each strategically meaningful. For the moment, we will focus on a couple of the key areas for illustration. Note that the basic benefit—"sound back to band is audible"—is in the middle area, labeled "Area B" or *points of parity*. The customer believes each of the two competing technologies delivers on that basic benefit. What distinguishes the Ultimate Ears product are the benefits in its Area A, that is, its *points of difference*. The product delivers substantial, unique value to customers in the form of superior performance (both due to hearing the performance better and less onstage equipment) and in substantially reducing hearing loss, a quality-of-life issue. It is difficult to identify any items that customers would call positive points of difference for the onstage monitors. In contrast, the *disequities* that were mentioned earlier fit into Area F, which is more broadly defined as disequities, or potential

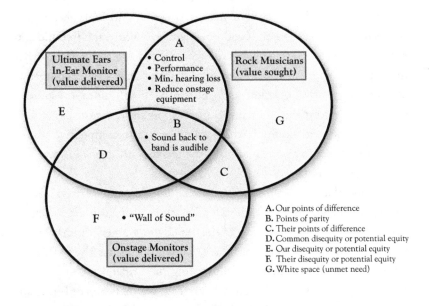

Figure 1.3. 3-Circle illustration of Ultimate Ears' competitive advantage.

equities, for the onstage monitor technology.[13] Ultimate Ears has been a major entrepreneurial success. This product concept, based on unique, patented technology and manufacturing capability, has become a standard in the industry. It creates significant customer benefits in both enhancing performance quality and the musicians' quality of life by limiting hearing loss.

The analysis based on Figures 1.1 through 1.3 illustrates that Ultimate Ears was successful because it

1. developed a unique *company capability*,
2. delivered value on a *customer need* that mattered greatly,
3. delivered that value in a manner that was superior to *competitive options*.

These are the three core principles of competitive business strategy that drive the analysis guided by the 3-Circle model.

Chapter Summary and Looking Ahead

While the 3-Circle analysis presented here provides a post-hoc account of Ultimate Ears' success after the fact, this book is about how to use the framework to analyze a current market situation and look ahead. The goal is to anticipate market development and evolution, and to build and execute solid growth strategy. We will see, in the chapters that follow, that this simple diagram provides a powerful basis for analysis of a company's current competitive position and substantial insight into prospective growth strategy for the company. But at its roots is the most basic of all competitive strategy notions—that in simplest terms, competitive advantage is about creating value that really matters for customers, in ways that competitors cannot.

We find that the most effective starting point for such analysis is the customer and developing a deep understanding of customers' values. Chapter 2 provides an overview of the underlying framework that begins with the customer perspective. There, we will introduce the basic concepts and several case examples illustrating the principles that underlie the development of effective growth strategy. We then proceed in chapters 3 through 8 to provide detail on the core model concepts. The process begins with a clear definition of context (chapter 3). It is followed by an in-depth study of customers in which we will deeply explore the value customers seek and how existing competitors get credit for the value they create (chapter 4). From these steps, significant insight is obtained into current competitive positions and potential growth. Chapter 5 presents the categorization of customer value that is at the heart of the 3-Circle model's contribution and in clarifying a firm's positioning. Chapter 6 then explores and defines the growth strategies that naturally evolve from the seven categories of value, leading to the inevitable question addressed in chapter 7: Do we have the skills and resources to pursue these ideas? Answering this requires a much deeper reflection on the firm's (and competitors') capabilities in terms of what strengths we have to leverage, what weaknesses we need to fix, and what gaps exist around which capability building will be necessary. Chapter 8 explores the dynamic aspects of markets and chapter 9 provides a summary of the book with a review of the 10-step process behind a 3-Circle growth strategy project.

This is designed to be a team process that engages customer, company, and competitor research in an integrative way. We look forward to the journey. At the end, you will find that the core of this analysis is seeking to deeply study and uncover ways to provide value for customers that competitors have simply not understood, and perhaps ways that have always been there for the taking. Chapter 2 next provides an overview of the full 3-Circle framework.

CHAPTER 2

Introduction to 3-Circle Analysis

Introduction

Booklet Binding, Inc., is a Chicago-based provider of finishing services for printers and publishers. The company provides folding, binding, cutting, and gluing services for printers preparing all forms of printed materials, including direct mail pieces. Started in 1976, the company distinguished itself from sleepy competitors by building fast service with the latest technology, making large gains in market share. By the mid-1990s, the competition had caught up. Customers increasingly saw the market as "commoditized," with competitors each believed to be delivering similar products with similar service levels. This led, much more quickly, to conversations about price and pressure to lower prices. In fact, this pressure became so significant that the company's salespeople began to introduce price into the conversation before customers even began to talk about it!

Commoditization is a real issue in most industries, as markets have become increasingly hypercompetitive and as competitive imitation of new ideas has become fast and furious. In this chapter, we will introduce the concepts in the 3-Circle model by considering customer value and how competitive forces evolve in a market, putting a premium on tools to understand that evolution. Commoditization is one of many strategic problems that is well addressed by the model.

Commoditization

There is a state in an industry in which all competitive products or services have evolved to look the same, that is, to appear undifferentiated. Investopedia defines commoditization as a situation in which "a product becomes indistinguishable from others like it and consumers buy on price alone."[1] As products or services become more similar in a market, there is an increasing reluctance among buyers to pay high prices. Picking up with our basic diagram from chapter 1, Figure 2.1 (part A) depicts a competitive market in which two different competitors (or competitor groups) show some degree of differentiation. Recall from Figure 1.3 in chapter 1 that Area B represents common value or "points of parity"—this is the value that customers believe both competitors provide. In contrast, Areas A and C capture what is unique about the two competitors. The firm in this example shows a healthy Area A and its competitor shows an equally healthy Area C, indicating that each firm is believed by customers to create unique value in ways the competitor does not. An example might be the market in which Booklet Binding, Inc., initially competed, where it created a distinctive position around service and speed that could not be matched by the smaller, traditional, competitive "craftsmen" in the industry, whose smaller size and longer customer relationships could differentiate them.

Fast-forward 15 years, and what you find is a market with a great deal of overlap in the value being provided by each competitor. Panel B of Figure 2.1 illustrates what happens in a commodity market. The predominant feature of this diagram is the enormous Area B, simply indicating that customers perceive a lot of common value. In other words, over time, the competitors have copied each other's advantages, and, as a result, they may largely be indistinguishable in the eyes of the customer—hence, the renewed focus on price to seek to gain customers' favor. Yet this often ends up in lost margin and blood on the income statement rather than competitive advantage.

The goal of this chapter is to introduce the 3-Circle model concepts in more depth, with the aim of illustrating how its primary goal of understanding how—in a market—value is perceived to be "shared" among competitors and how it is actually created. As it turns out, the primary way out of commoditization is through deeply exploring customer value in order to

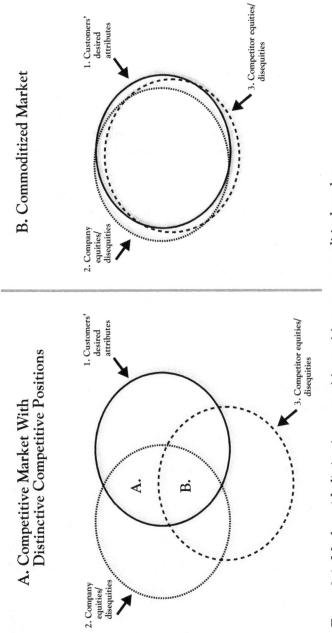

Figure 2.1. Market with distinctive competitive positions vs. commoditized market.

identify and understand needs that have not been well articulated. This is one of the core insights of the 3-Circle growth strategy process.

Some Fundamentals

The easiest—and, in fact, most powerful—definition of *customer value* is that it is the customer's sense of *what benefits they get from a firm relative to the price they pay*. There is a way to quantify this, which we will see. But the fact is that most firms use the term loosely, without much precision—a topic of some consideration in chapter 4. It is a term that seems to have intuitive meaning to people, which can be dangerous. One manager might be talking about the quality of a product, while another may be thinking about price. But each is defining this under the rubric "value." We will provide a more formal definition of customer value shortly, but first consider why the concept of customer value is important in the first place.

Customer Value and Financial Value

The best way to answer the question of why customer value is important is to think about how customer value plays into the bottom line of the firm. Global customer value expert Ray Kordupleski has an excellent chapter in his book *Mastering Customer Value Management* that goes to great lengths to illustrate very strong relationships among measures of customer value perceptions, market share, and profitability.[2] The truth is that firms create financial value most effectively by first focusing on the value they create for customers. At the highest level, it is easy to illustrate that profit is a function of revenue and cost:

$$profit = total\ revenue - total\ cost.$$

Further, total revenue can be broken down as a function of volume and price:

$$total\ revenue = Q * price,$$

where Q is equal to the sales volume of the product or service (how many units we sell) and price is how much we charge customers for it.

Then, a simple way to think about Q (how much we can sell) is that it is determined by customers' choices. First, we sell more when more customers choose our brand over competitive brands. Second, the reason customers will tend to choose our brand over competitors is that they believe our brand is a better value for the money.

Frank Perdue

So think of chicken.[3] Twenty years ago, chicken was a commodity product in the grocery store. Different brands were perceived to be very similar and were sold at similar prices. Perdue chicken was one of those brands. Considering the definition of value given previously, we can envision a scenario that defines a commodity market:

$$\frac{\text{benefits from Perdue chicken}}{\text{price of Perdue chicken}} = \frac{\text{benefits from brand z}}{\text{price of brand z}} \quad ,$$

where the ratios can be thought of as capturing each brand's value for the money ("was that product or service worth what I paid for it?"). If the two ratios are equal, you have a commodity market. It is a coin flip to determine which brand a consumer will choose.

In the face of this situation, Frank Perdue did something to change this market. Based on a study of the value that customers sought from chicken, Perdue concluded that consumers wanted meatier, yellower chicken, with no pinfeathers. He then put significant research and investment into breeding and technology that would produce plumper chickens with yellower skin, and processing with turbine engine blow-drying to remove pin feathers on the skin. Essentially, Perdue substantially increased the *numerator* in his value ratio, greatly enhancing the benefits that consumers received from his chicken. A creative advertising program further enhanced those benefits by communicating the uniqueness of Perdue chicken and conveying Perdue's no-nonsense personality. At equivalent prices, the Perdue brand became a clear choice for the consumer of the competitive brand Z because it delivers more effectively on important consumer benefits sought.

Considering the relative value ratios, although the denominators are essentially the same, the Perdue numerator is larger, making the overall ratio larger. Interestingly, though, as Perdue's sales grew as a result of the improved product, competitive brands began to reduce their prices to try to defend their market shares. Yet many consumers still stuck with the higher-priced Perdue brand, meaning they were willing to trade-off higher prices for better chicken. In sum, even at a higher price point, Perdue's benefits were still considered to be a good *value for the money*. This was the foundation for Perdue chicken establishing a very profitable niche in the retail grocery market.

So, to this point, a few fundamentals are important:

- Customers choose products or services that they believe provide greater value.
- Commoditization occurs as, over time, firms imitate new ideas and the products and services (and value ratios) become increasingly similar.
- Breaking out of commoditization requires a focus on customer value and the reasons why customers choose certain products. A firm can distinguish its offering by either substantively enhancing the benefits offered or lowering the customer's costs in a way that is difficult to imitate.
- Greater customer value relative to the competition produces more sales volume, greater revenue, and greater profit (provided it is created within a manageable cost structure).

The Outside View

The 3-Circle model provides a method of explicitly identifying the current state of customer value in a market and a variety of sources for improving a firm's competitive position and profit potential. In introducing the 3-Circle model here, in chapter 2, we will first take you through what we refer to as the "outside" view. This represents the customer's view of the world. Yet it is important to briefly distinguish this outside view and what we later refer to as the inside view.

The *outside view* is what customers believe about us. The outside view is the front office or maybe even the front window. It captures the impressions our customers, and potential customers, have about us based on what they observe: seeing and using our products and services, our pricing, distributor relationships, exposure to our marketing communications and to word-of-mouth from others familiar with us, and so on. The outside view is the *customer's perception* of our value and competitors' value. It is the rock musician's beliefs about the Ultimate Ears monitors and the benefits he or she derives from them.

In contrast, the *inside view* is the back office. It is what we really are on the inside—the assets, resources, capabilities, and knowledge that we bring to bear in producing value for customers. The inside view is what we really are and can do. For Ultimate Ears, this reflects the true capability the company has for research and development, product design, manufacturing, sales, and customer relationship management in serving the market.

The distinction between outside and inside is very important. We will learn that there are many, many times that customers' view of a company does not match the actual value that the company is creating or can create. Further, as George Day of the Wharton School first suggested, true competitive advantage occurs only when the distinctive value produced for customers is produced by real capabilities and assets that competitors cannot match.[4]

The DNA of Customer Value: Attributes

We will formalize this discussion in chapter 4, but our first premise is that customers purchase and consume value in the form of product attributes. Derived from the Latin root *attributus* (which means "to bestow"), the word *attribute* means an inherent characteristic or a quality of some object. In the same way that people can be described as a bundle of characteristics (height, weight, gender, ethnicity, age), goods and services can be described based on size, cost, quality, reliability, and reputation.

In fact, it is surprising how precisely we can characterize the attributes or features of products and services. We started with a relatively simple description of chicken—with dimensions of meatiness, color, presence of pin feathers, and price. More complex product categories (e.g., dishwashers) might have over 100 attributes when functional qualities, design qualities, pre- and postpurchase services, and perception of transactional factors are taken into account. Table 2.1 (column 1) provides a partial list of the attributes of cell phones to illustrate how value can be broken down into component parts.

Table 2.1. Customer Values for Cellular Telephones

Features/form	Benefits: Usefulness	Benefits: Other
Features • Has a screen • Has easily readable text • Has a memory • Has a directory • Can connect to a computer • Is data capable • Size • Weight • Talk time • Standby time • Battery life • Button size • Mode (single, double, triple band) • Has flip top • Screen size • Memory size • Directory size • Number of characters displayed on screen • Has a working antennae **Form** • Is fashionable • Is slick • Is thin • Is shiny • Comes with colored face plates • Looks good	**Enhance voice communication** • Voice mail • Two-way radio • Allows group calls • Has caller ID • Has vibration alert • Has a speaker phone • Has speed dialing • Can adjust volume dynamically • Has a phone directory • Stores recently phoned numbers • Stores recent incoming phone numbers • Missed called indicator • Has voice recorder **Enhance Text Communication** • E-mail • Has alphanumeric paging **Facilitate Cost Management** • Indicates cost of a completed call • Monitors monthly usage **Enhance Personal Organization** • Personal calendar • Puts address info in PDA • Provides reminders to users • Indicates time • Has an alarm • Has a clock • Has a calculator **Provide for Internet Use** • Internet access • Web access **Has Games**	**Durability** • Be rugged • Be reliable • Not easy to break **Comfort** • Feels good • Fits face • Fits hand **Socially acceptable** • Popular • Consistent with profession • Consistent with position • Consistent with peers **Ease of Use** • Simple to program • Easy to maintain (e.g., charge battery) • Easy to use telephone • Easy access (belt clip, fits in pocket) • Hard to lose **Safety** • While driving a vehicle • From regular use • In emergencies **Cost** • Cost of phone • Cost of accessories

Note. Adapted from "Stimulating creative design alternatives using customer values," by R. L. Keeney, 2004, *IEEE Transactions on Systems, Man, and Cybernetics-Part C: Applications and Reviews, 34,* 50–459.

Sorting Value

The first fundamental insight of the 3-Circle model is that we can learn a lot about firms' positions in a market by sorting the attributes in a way that clarifies customer beliefs about which competitors get credit for which attributes and benefits. The framework provides a strategically meaningful way to categorize current attributes and anticipate the creation of future value. An organization gets insight into its current and future competitive position by examining how value can be broken down into attributes, determining how important those attributes are, and identifying what attributes customers associate most strongly with each competitor.

What follows is an illustration of the *output* of a 3-Circle analysis. For the illustration, we use the case of a small church-based primary school. Although one might believe education to be a commoditized market, in fact, the analysis reveals some interesting, very natural differences in competitive positions. It is also important to note that the analysis here is based on the same exercise in examining growth strategy as one would undertake in any competitive market. While the focus again is on output here, subsequent chapters will provide detail on *process*.

Context

Glenview New Church is a religious organization in Glenview, Illinois, headed by Pastor Peter Buss. The church has a small primary school for kindergarten through 8th grade. With the school still early in its development, Pastor Buss undertook a 3-Circle analysis in the interest of building growth strategy. Pastor Buss focused on parishioners, parents of younger school-aged children as the *market segment* to study, and the Glenview Public Schools as the *competitive target*. The goal of a 3-Circle analysis is to build a growth strategy for Glenview New Church School (GNCS) via a deep study of the customer's view of competitive positions (outside view) and an internal analysis of the school's current capabilities and assets (inside view). We begin with the outside view.

Customer Circle

Having identified the target customer segment for the analysis as young parishioner families with school-aged children, we can depict the customer circle as reflecting the value they seek. What are the attributes of schools that affect family choices? There are several that are straightforward:

- Where is the school located (e.g., how far from my house)?
- What is the quality of the education there?
- Do they have good teachers?
- What are the other families like?

These are some of the basic criteria families will use to evaluate the schools they are considering.

A more complete listing of attributes that emerged from the analysis is given in Figure 2.2. These attributes and considerations are determined by conversations with the target segment. These concerns are familiar, relating to curriculum, quality of teaching, school culture, facilities, and so on. The list is generated from thoughtfully listening to people describe how and why they *chose* their school or are *considering their choice of schools*. Of course, not all of these factors are considered by all families. Some factors are more important than others. In fact, we can usually group customers together in terms of the factors that are most important in their decision making. These groups are called market segments, and such groups will be considered in more depth in chapter 3. For the moment, we will summarize the area of the customer circle as capturing the value a particular customer segment is seeking—in other words, what the customers want.

Customer Circle: What are the "attributes" that influence families' decision making for schools?

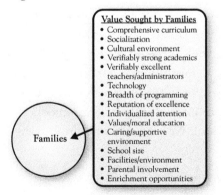

Figure 2.2. Glenview New Church School: Customer circle.

Company Circle

In Figure 2.3, we add a circle that represents the customer's perception of how well our company (in this case, Glenview New Church School) is delivering on the value that the customer is seeking. At this point, it is very important to distinguish the fact that the circle represents *customer perception*—it does not represent what we actually offer or what we think we offer. This distinction is critical in emphasizing that the outside view focuses on *what customers believe* rather than what we (the firm) believe the reality to be.

As we know from chapter 1, bringing these two circles together produces the simple distinction between positive value (the overlapping area), nonvalue or negative value, and unmet needs.

Pastor Buss discovered that families recognized the school for its comprehensive curriculum, for a caring and supportive environment, and for a value- and morals-based education. In addition, they felt that the school facility met their needs, including availability of after-school enrichment programs and parental involvement. We will expand upon the other two areas (nonvalue or negative value and unmet needs) as we build the analysis out. Suffice to say that there are a number of positives that Pastor

Company Circle: GNCS is believed to create value in many ways.

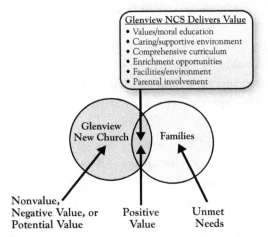

Figure 2.3. Glenview New Church School: Adding the company circle.

Buss heard from families. Yet the surprise in this analysis occurs when we subsequently learn that our competitor not only has many of the same positives, they also have some positives that *we don't have*! So the next step is to add a circle that represents customer perception of the competitor, in this case, Glenview Public Schools.

Competitor Circle and Areas A, B, and C
Among other competitors for GNCS, Glenview Public School District 34 (GPSD) is formidable. Glenview has a total enrollment of over 4,300 students across 3 primary, 3 intermediate, and 2 middle schools. Four of the schools have been selected as National Blue Ribbon schools. There are 370 teachers, with an average of 8 years teaching experience, three-quarters of whom have a master's degree. What are the beliefs of parents regarding the value provided by the Glenview public school system?

Figure 2.4 introduces the competitor circle, illustrating some very important distinctions. First, one striking point is that of all the dimensions of positive value for GNCS depicted in Figure 2.2, *only about half are unique* to Pastor Buss's school relative to the competitor (individualized attention, values- and moral-based education, and caring and supportive environment, which define GNCS's Area A, or *points of difference*). The attributes on which GNCS is believed to be about the same as GPSD are comprehensive curriculum, facilities, enrichment (after-school programs), and parental involvement. This latter set of attributes is labeled *Points of Parity* (**Area B**), as the competitors are "at parity"—that is, neither is believed to have a unique advantage. In other frameworks, these dimensions are given other labels (e.g., table stakes; expected product) but have the same basic meaning. These are the factors that customers fundamentally expect all schools to deliver on in order to be in the consideration set.

What was striking to Pastor Buss, however, was to identify the points of difference for GPSD, the competitor (**Area C**). GPSD got a great deal of credit for the breadth of its curriculum, its technology, its greater opportunity for socialization among a diverse population, and its reputation. But one dimension that surprised Pastor Buss and his team was the heavy weight that parents placed on the notion of "verifiability" in both academic performance and teacher credentials. This weight is consistent

Competitor Circle: Some values are common (Area B) and unique (Areas A and C)

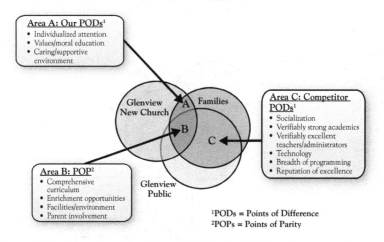

Area A: Our PODs[1]
- Individualized attention
- Values/moral education
- Caring/supportive environment

Glenview New Church   A   Families

Area C: Competitor PODs[1]
- Socialization
- Verifiably strong academics
- Verifiably excellent teachers/administrators
- Technology
- Breadth of programming
- Reputation of excellence

B

C

Area B: POP[2]
- Comprehensive curriculum
- Enrichment opportunities
- Facilities/environment
- Parent involvement

Glenview Public

[1]PODs = Points of Difference
[2]POPs = Points of Parity

Figure 2.4. Glenview New Church School: Adding the competitor circle.

with the attention that standardized testing has received since the passage of the No Child Left Behind Act of 2001 (NCLBA), requiring performance standards for adequate yearly progress for public schools. Illinois private schools such as GNCS are not subject to the same performance standards and are therefore not required to administer standardized tests. Pastor Buss discovered that standardized test scores as evidence of academic performance were a major positive point of difference for Glenview Public—and therefore a disequity for GNCS.

The Meanings of Areas D, E, and F

Figure 2.5 focuses on the areas of the model that, for both firms, fall *outside* the customer's circle. By definition, these areas reflect the firms' attributes and benefits that are unimportant to customers or do not meet customer needs. **Areas D**, **E**, and **F** capture value that is being produced by the competitive firms that fits into one of two categories:

- *Nonvalue: Value that is unimportant to customers.* This could include attributes that were once differentiating but became points-of-parity and have lost their value over time. For

Areas D, E, and F: Nonvalue, Negative Value, or Potential Value for Each School

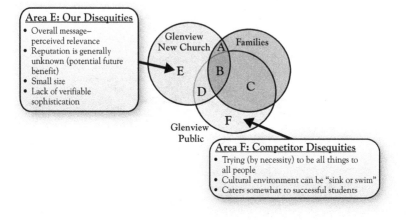

Figure 2.5. *Glenview New Church School: Areas of nonvalue, negative value (disequities), or potential value.*

example, at one time, batteries had self-testers built right into the packages so that users could see how much life was left at any point they wanted. This was an attribute that initially differentiated Duracell, but it turned out to be an expensive add-on imitated by competitors that did not provide substantial enough incremental value to customers to justify its existence. Alternatively, certain attributes are simply pushed out by superior technology—for example, at one time, golf clubs called "woods" were actually made of wood! Finally, nonvalue can also include attributes or benefits that firms *thought* would create value for customers but, in the end, did not. Handwriting recognition on personal digital assistants (PDAs), colas of a clear color, and separate boy and girl disposable diapers were all efforts that firms anticipated would be big sellers but that consumers found to demonstrate little incremental value.

- *Negative value (disequity): Value with which customers are dissatisfied.* We might also find negative value in these areas. This might alternatively be referred to as dissatisfiers or "disequities."

Industry-wide dissatisfiers fall into Area D—both (or maybe all) competitors suffer from this. Some might say that customer service in the airline industry is very poor across all or most competitors. Alternatively, one firm may possess a dissatisfier while another does not. Major retail video stores continue to charge fees for late returns, for example, which is a major source of customer dissatisfaction in the video rental industry. In contrast, competitor Netflix has a business model that does not require customers to pay late fees. The alarm clock that works fine but is very difficult to set, the mobile phone service that has good coverage but for which billing is complex and confusing, and good physicians with long wait times are all examples of products and services for which we accept the good and the bad. That is, consumers essentially trade-off the positive returns from consumption in these categories against the negative returns that, in some cases, they simply decide to put up with.

In the case of Glenview New Church School, the public school's strength in verifiable academic performance is actually a unique disequity, which would define it as falling into Area E. Simply, parents have a more difficult time choosing a school in a post-NCLBA world if the evidence of performance is not offered up. The notion of verifiability both in terms of school performance and staff credentials was something of a surprise to the GNCS management team. In his study, Pastor Buss's analysis for GNCS did not reveal any items of common disequity (Area D) for the two schools.

In addition, Pastor Buss was surprised to hear that many parents were not clear on the church's mission for the new school. There were two dimensions of this. First, the reputation of the school was generally unknown among some parents. Second, some of those who were aware of the school conveyed that the church's communications about the school were not perceived as relevant—that is, they did not personally connect with the messages. The sum total of these two concerns is that the school's identity was difficult to pin down, which can be a disequity in the customer's eyes.

As we will see, these areas turn out to be very important, in part because there are strategic options for dealing with these concerns that have implications for growth. Attributes or benefits one finds in Area E, for example, might be (a) maintained, (b) eliminated to save cost, or, ironically, (c) actually built into potential satisfiers.

Area G: The White Space

Innovation is a critical component of growth strategy for many organizations today. As such, it is critical to have a systematic way of motivating the search for new customer value ideas. The 3-Circle model gives meaning and language to the need for innovation.

Figure 2.6 focuses on **Area G**, which we label the "white space."[5] This region of the framework actually has two different dimensions or meanings, both critically important. The white space generically captures value desired by the customer that is not currently being fulfilled by either the firm or its competitor. Those needs may be (a) currently known and top-of-mind or (b) less known (latent). Needs that are currently known and top-of-mind are often obvious in customer complaints; therefore, many clues about unmet needs might be found in the attributes that end up in areas D, E, and F. For example, the travel industry is complex and rife with consumer dissatisfaction due to late planes, mistaken communications, and confusing airline loyalty programs, among other factors.[6] In

Area G: Digging deeper reveals customer needs that are unmet or could be met more effectively.

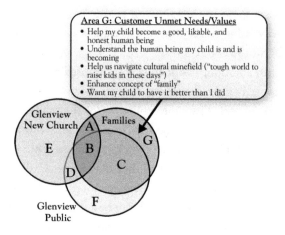

Figure 2.6. Glenview New Church School: Area G, unmet needs.

short, there may be needs the customer has that are known and that have not yet been satisfied.

Yet there are also underlying needs that may be less obvious. As we will discuss in chapters 5 and 6, there are approaches for exploring the white space that require deeper inquiry, and a variety of methods are available. To illustrate this distinction, notice the last two columns of Table 2.1. While the first column deals explicitly with the *features* of the phone itself, the second and third columns focus on the *outcomes* of particular features of the phone. So, for example, while the packaging and sales discussion might focus on a number of features like screen readability, size, weight, and battery and memory size, ultimately, the customer wants to get a sense of how this phone will help them in voice and text communication, personal organization, durability, safety, and comfort. The latter reflects deeper needs, which might more powerfully guide product development by providing a clearer understanding of customer problems to be solved.

In his analysis of GNCS parents' decision making regarding schools, Pastor Buss utilized a research approach called "laddering," which effectively drills down into deeper reasons underlying customers interest in the attributes of a product or service. So why are attributes like individualized attention, comprehensive curriculum, and values-based curriculum important to families as they choose among schools? Figure 2.6 reveals several interesting values that Pastor Buss identified in his in-depth conversations with customers. These values relate to the deeper goals that parents have for their children—becoming a likable, honest person; navigating a cultural minefield; wanting their child to have it better than they did. These are not attributes of the school but are ultimately outcomes of the school's attributes. They are unmet in the sense that they probably can never be completely resolved. At the same time, the school's efforts to speak to these values in program development, hiring, and communications will have a very big impact on the value that parents find in the school.

Note that these deeper values are hardwired in us. No firm "creates" needs—they are built into us and drive our daily behaviors. However, most of us as consumers (and as managers) do not really think about these deeper drivers on a regular basis. But recognizing their existence—by keeping a focus on Area G in growth strategy planning—can offer dramatic insight into customer value and impact on growth strategy. An example is a case involving the Rust-Oleum management team.

Rust-Oleum is a well-known manufacturer of high quality paints, with its brand anchored around its historically highly effective rust-preventative paints. Facing pressure from retail store category managers to lower prices, company management found deeper concerns about category profitability (and, likely, personal achievement) in the retail category managers' protests. Instead of cutting prices, the Rust-Oleum team sought to more deeply understand the problem that category managers were attempting to solve. They concluded that the retailers' *real issue* was not a need to extract more margin from individual vendors but, instead, a need to *improve the overall profitability of their small project paint category*. In response, Rust-Oleum created a data-driven approach to category management for small project paints, helping retailers significantly improve sales and profit from the paint category and producing double-digit growth in sales of its own brand.

The lesson is that in any product or service category, needs are never completely fulfilled. Area G is a critically important source of potential value to be added in a market that can fuel growth. It is important to note that Pastor Buss's analysis of GNCS was undertaken on his own, with guidance from the 10-step 3-Circle growth strategy process that is summarized in chapter 9 of this book. We will discuss the implications of this analysis for the school's growth strategy, but we will first consider the concept of the inside view.

The Inside View

In 3-Circle analysis, significant insight is gained by thinking of the circles as having deeper layers. For example, Pastor Buss found that at the core of parents' decisions about schools was a deep concern about their child's development as an honest human being and achievement in later life. Similarly, the company circle has depth to it. That is, residing behind or inside the company circle that customers see are the capabilities, resources, assets, and value networks that the firm uses to create value for its customers.[7]

Capabilities, Resources, and Assets

Figure 2.7 provides a simple schematic of the dimensions on which the inside view might be discussed. The circle on the left results from an analysis of our company's resources, capabilities, and assets (which we will refer to as RCA). The circle would "contain" a weighted listing of our RCAs, to be compared to those of the competitor, captured by the circle on the right. Note that the two circles overlap, which suggest that the firms have some capabilities in common. Yet each firm has unique RCAs as well.

This brings us to the ultimate definition of distinctive *competitive advantage* (following the work of Michael Porter and George Day). True competitive advantage exists when the attributes or benefits that reside in Area A in the outside view of the model (seen by customers) are the product of the firm's *unique* RCAs. In other words, the strongest, most sustainable competitive advantage is one in which the firm's unique position in the mind of customers (Area A) is produced by capabilities and resources that competitors cannot match.

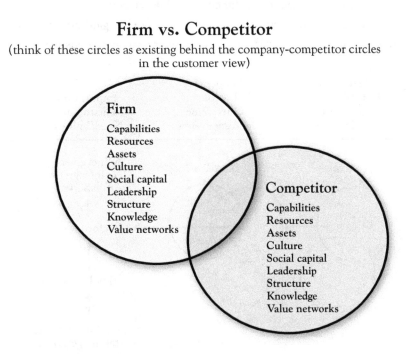

Firm vs. Competitor
(think of these circles as existing behind the company-competitor circles
in the customer view)

Firm
Capabilities
Resources
Assets
Culture
Social capital
Leadership
Structure
Knowledge
Value networks

Competitor
Capabilities
Resources
Assets
Culture
Social capital
Leadership
Structure
Knowledge
Value networks

Figure 2.7. The inside view.

Competitive Advantage and Red Bull

At the heart of the framework is the idea that true competitive advantage comes from aligning the firm's distinctive RCA to important customer values in ways that competitors do not. To illustrate, consider Red Bull, the brand that pioneered the "functional energy drink" beverage category. Figure 2.8 illustrates, in simple terms, the idea of alignment. The company built a variety of distinctive capabilities around research and development, product development, and (later) branding and marketing communications. Based on these capabilities, the company developed unique strategies for product (a research-based formula including the newly introduced ingredient taurine), distribution (refrigeration units and display innovation in retail stores, building relationships with clubs), and promotion (sponsorship or creation of high-energy events and athletes). These tactics were driven by the Area A positioning strategy "revitalizing body and mind," ultimately delivering uniquely on the basic needs of combating mental and physical fatigue in people seeking performance, achievement, or socialization. IBISWorld reports that, as of 2010, Red Bull has a 70% share of the "energy drink" segment of the functional drink category.[8]

The Red Bull case illustrates an important point regarding a common misconception about what most people believe to be vacuous marketing

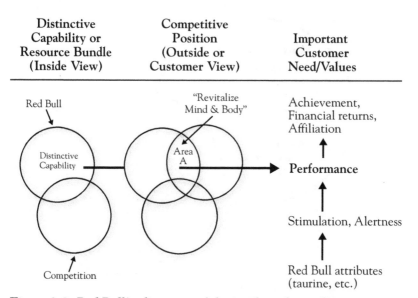

Figure 2.8. Red Bull's alignment of the inside and outside views.

practices as a key to marketplace success. Without the foundation capabilities and resources in execution, communications campaign seek to create image are doomed to fail. The most successful brands and products are those that deliver on the promises made in positioning via strong core capabilities. In describing the history, structure, philosophy, and success of the Mayo Clinic—one of the most successful and important enterprises in American business history—Len Berry and Kent Selman (2008) note, "Smart executives understand that advertising effectiveness over time depends on advertised goods or services delivering what the organization promises." In sum, the brand is a result of performance of the product or service. For Glenview New Church School, capability development is critical. GNCS's current Area A is essentially built around its small size, individualized attention, and morals-based education. As we will see, there are opportunities for developing growth strategy that are based upon building new capabilities.

Growth Strategies

The most significant contribution of the 3-Circle model is the guidance on growth strategy that falls relatively easily out of an effective customer analysis. We will use the GNCS example to quickly illustrate this. First, recall our basic definition of customer value:

$$\text{value} = \frac{\text{benefits obtained}}{\text{price paid}}.$$

As noted, this ratio is important in suggesting that the firm increases the chance that the potential customer will choose their brand when they either increase the numerator relative to the competition or reduce the denominator. Apple and Dell represent polar opposites in terms of competitive positions—Apple differentiated around excellent design and functionality (with margin driving its profitability) and Dell focused more on efficiency, low-cost basis, and aggressive pricing (with high volume driving its profitability). In some ways—and with certain exceptions—we might refer to Apple as a numerator company and Dell as a denominator company. Each creates significant value for its customers but in very different ways.

As a self-funded private school, GNCS does charge tuition. It gives regular parishioners a discount from the stated tuition level. For the purposes of our discussion here, we will not introduce a tuition cut into the mix for GNCS. However, it is important to note that price reduction—when financially well reasoned—is a plausible alternative here, particularly if it is accompanied by cost reductions.

We will organize the consideration of growth strategies around four questions. Although we will later see that there are additional growth strategy implications that emerge from the model, these four questions are most fundamental.

Growth Question 1: How Do We Build and Defend Area A?

The 3-Circle model makes a fundamental premise of competitive strategy very plain: The firm must be different from competitors in ways that matter to customers. One of the most valuable aspects of the model is the manager's ability to teach colleagues and staff this notion. But beyond just conveying understanding of the notion that all firms must have points of difference to grow there are important implications in (a) first discovering our points of difference from the customer's perspective (often, they are not what we expect) and then (b) thinking through how we can build and defend them. In a subsequent chapter, we will detail the bases for differentiation and the variety of ways that firms attack this important element of strategy. For the GNCS example, growth question 1 is summarized in Figure 2.9.

Although relatively new, GNCS does have a differential advantage over the public schools in its small size, caring environment, and potential for individualized attention to children. These are natural advantages, but the team at GNCS decided that they could be leveraged in two ways. These two secondary questions form a foundation for growth strategy in each of the general categories we will discuss:

- *What capabilities can we build to reinforce and strengthen our Area A?* In education, there is an important paradigm developing around what is known as differentiated instruction.[9] This teaching pedagogy focuses on teaching children in a way that adapts to their individual differences in learning styles and levels. The approach requires training and development for teachers that is not standard in colleges of education. One

How do we identify, build, and defend differentiation that is meaningful to customers?

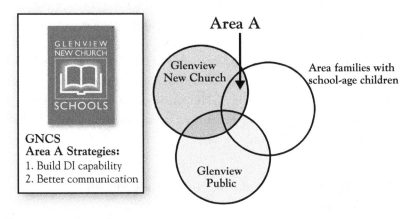

Figure 2.9. Growth question 1.

growth direction for GNCS is to build teacher skill sets in differentiated instruction, which the public schools would have a more difficult time pursuing.

- *Can we communicate more effectively?* Pastor Buss did discover in his research, to his surprise, that several families were unaware of the school's value proposition and how it related to their values. There is an important opportunity here to better connect messages about the school's positioning to the values uncovered in the Area G analysis.

Growth Question 2: How Do We Correct, Reduce, or Eliminate Disequity and Build Potential Equities in Area E?

Figure 2.10 identifies a series of questions about Area E, which we only summarize here and save for greater depth later. In some ways, this is even a higher short-term priority than building Area A. Very often in this analysis, firms find that customers raise concerns that they were not aware of, and find that these concerns are sometimes based on misconceptions. Again, GNCS discovered a general lack of awareness of the school's value proposition. The clear growth strategy emerging from this is conducting an audit of all communications media and touch-points, as well as all opportunities to clearly convey the school's mission and, again, how it connects to the Area G values identified. Probably the most significant disequity defined for GNCS was the fact that they lacked the test scores that would provide credible evidence of both the school's academic excellence and the teaching staff's credentials, the former because the school had not undertaken the standardized tests and the latter because they had never thought to communicate teacher credentials. In their analysis, GNCS discovered the importance of building a capability in standardized testing and in very clearly promoting their teachers' advanced degrees.

Growth Question 3: Should We Neutralize Competitors' Area C, and If So, How?

In Area C reside the competitors' strengths. Growth for our firm may be produced by offsetting or neutralizing these perceived advantages for the competitor (Figure 2.11). One can see the complementary relationship between Areas C and E here—the competitor's advantages (Area C) may, at times, be seen as the firm's disequities (Area E). The issue of whether

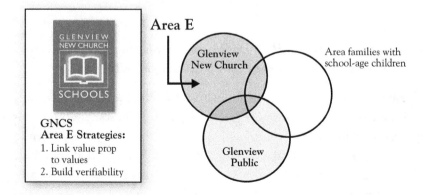

How do we correct, reduce/eliminate disequities, or reveal equities that customers are unaware of?

Figure 2.10. Growth question 2.

or not the firm should vigorously attack Area C depends—to what degree do we have, or can we build, a credible attack on the competitor? What are the costs of, and returns from, such an attack? In the case of GNCS, neutralizing the public school's advantage on verifiability (i.e., building the standardized testing capability) is straightforward. This is essentially a competitive requirement today, because test scores are data that families expect each school to be able to produce (i.e., it has essentially become a point of parity). In addition, the costs of building this capability are reasonable, particularly compared to the costs of *not* doing it. As noted, though, the firm needs to be discriminating about which Area C dimensions to attack. Given resource constraints and a more focused mission, it would not make sense for GNCS to seek to broaden its curriculum to match the curriculum breadth of GPSD, for example.

A related growth strategy question that falls roughly into the category of growth question 3 is the question of whether or not to attack or leverage the competitor's disequities (Area F). To the extent that such deficiencies are strategically important (i.e., associated or potentially associated with customer value), these dimensions represent an opportunity to directly attack the competition to take away customers. Overcoming deficiencies involves making better products or services than

Should we neutralize competitors' differentiation? If so, how?

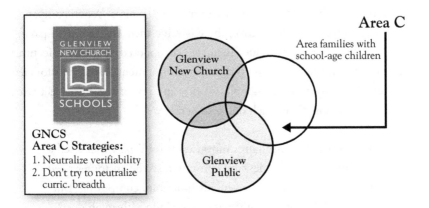

Figure 2.11. Growth question 3.

the competition and distributing them more effectively. In addition, communications strategy can point out the problems with the competitor's offerings. Research on comparative advertising suggests that a direct attack on a smaller competitor is generally a bad idea for a market leader. But the fact that it may work for an underdog is reflected in Apple's brilliant "Get a Mac" campaign, which cleverly and effectively positioned Microsoft as an overconfident (if insecure), bumbling nerd of a competitor.

Growth Question 4: How Can We Identify Totally New Growth Ideas in Area G?

Customers' needs are never fully met. There are always problems somewhere in the customer's consumption chain for which alternative solutions might be developed that could serve to ultimately build Area A. This includes both functional value (e.g., suitcases with wheels and golf bags with stand-up legs are only recent inventions in a long history of travel and golf), and deeper psychological or social value (e.g., helping parents feel more confident about the chances for their children's future success). To illustrate, consider the human value "control." Deep-seated and highly influential in guiding our behavior, the desire for control is what is called an *instrumental* value. That means that it is an intermediary of a value— that is, it helps lead to other terminal values like peace of mind or security.[10] But the overriding point is straightforward: *We value feeling in control.* In general, humans like to feel a sense of certainty and predictability. Through evolution, this has just been hardwired into our systems. When companies can help us feel more in control, there is value there that is worth paying for. Thinking about the values (control), as opposed to product features and attributes, tends to open up thinking about potential solutions for customers. It is easy to find examples of new innovations that connect with customers because they touch our *sense of control*:

- *Palm Pilot.* This brilliant innovation was initially marketed as a competitor to the desktop computer, so the customer need was envisioned to be convenient (portable) computing. But founder Jeff Hawkins ultimately concluded (through deeper research with users) that the PDA was essentially a device

not for computing per se but for helping business people get
control of their information, schedule, and personal contacts,
and for subsequent performance on the job. Users believe that
PDAs are superior to paper-based planning systems like Day-
Timer for this purpose.

- *Global positioning systems (GPS).* According to marketing
  researcher RNCOS, GPS products and applications sales will be
  $75 billion by 2013.[11] From helping farmers maximize crop yields,
  to helping companies track shipping fleets, to helping golfers find
  the yardage to the hole, this technology is going a long way toward
  enhancing our sense of control over the physical environment.

- *Calorie management websites.* As evidence mounts that the
  key principle in weight reduction is simply managing caloric
  intake,[12] a wide variety of websites have popped up that help
  people track the number of calories they take in and burn up
  every day, including SparkPeople, LIVESTRONG, and About.
  com Health. These services bring a strong element of control
  by way of enhancing one's ability to monitor and regulate eating behavior with some advising—a self-regulatory solution to
  what is often an emotional, fad-driven activity.

We will expand our discussion of values in chapter 4, but, for now, we
point out that the exploration of Area G for growth opportunities requires
going beyond the current conception of the product or service. It requires a
way of exploring customers' deeper problems, needs, and motives.

At the chapter's opening, we discussed Booklet Binding, Inc. (BBI), the
firm competing in the market for printed booklets that had become commoditized. After deeper study of customers' purchasing patterns and needs,
the company turned itself around by listening more carefully to individual
customer needs and by expanding the definition of its product. It found
that customers would significantly benefit from sales programs that anticipated their promotion schedules over time, reminded them of previous
orders, and helped them plan ahead. It also found that they could create
value for customers through education on topics that helped customers improve their efficiency and sales effectiveness. These efforts not only
enhanced customers' sense of control over at least one aspect of their business, it also helped BBI customers create more value for *their* customers.

This required redefining what BBI considered to be its core product and service capabilities, but in doing so, the company was able to recapture a substantial part of the market and to improve profitability.

Regarding GNCS, we have already made some mention of the values that Pastor Buss uncovered in Area G. Given this depth of understanding of the values driving family school choice, the GNCS team should evaluate all existing programs in terms of how well they deliver upon these values (see Figure 2.12). Subsequently, the team should strive to build the programs that most directly address these values and perhaps eliminate programs that do not. So an after-school program that can be understood to have the benefits of preparing primary school students for middle school is likely to have a greater impact than one that has a more general positioning. New programs might be built specifically around the life skills that contribute to the children's ability to navigate challenging circumstances, like decision-making skills.[13] Finally, it is important for GNCS to reflect these values in their communication with prospects.

Chapter Summary

Pastor Buss and the GNCS team are still working on implementing the strategic directions that emerged from the 3-Circle project. They have

How can we identify totally new growth ideas around customers' unmet needs?

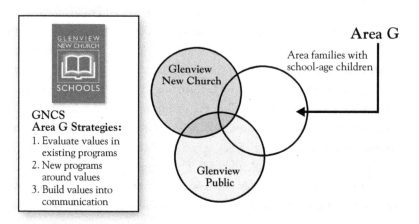

Figure 2.12. Growth question 4.

built an impressive staff and communicated their cred|
mented standardized testing processes, and are in the pr|
new leadership. While the development of the school will|
the development of new teaching paradigms like differer|
tion will be up to the new school leaders, Pastor Buss reports being "sold
on the 3-Circle model" and process that led to the current growth strategy for the school.

The simple truth is that your business is more profitable when you
lead it with a careful view to customer value. However, there is much
lip service given to customer value and customer satisfaction these days
because we have few disciplined ways to think about and evaluate it. The
3-Circle model provides such discipline in asking the right questions and
providing guidance on the right answers for growth. The key benefits of
the framework are the following:

- Understanding the customer's perspective with a focus on competitive assessment and the deeper values underlying customer
  decision making
- Straightforward illustration of principles of competitive strategy and actionable implications for how to improve competitive position
- An explicit focus on building competitive advantage through
  both capability development and communications strategy

The outside view of the framework captures the *front office*—that is, it
focuses explicitly on customer perception of the firm and its competitor.
The analysis of the outside view produces a categorization of value in 7
categories, as summarized in Figure 2.13. The key competitive concepts
reflected in this figure, and the associated growth strategy implications,
are as follows:

- **Area A**: *Our* competitive points of difference. Build and
  defend.
- **Area B**: Points of parity. This is the common value that
  customers may come to expect from all competitors. These
  attributes and benefits should generally be monitored and
  maintained at competitive levels.

- **Area C:** *Their* (the competitor's) points of difference. If there are absolutely critical dimensions that can be matched in cost-effective ways, there is a high priority on matching the competitor's advantages. The exception is when the competitor's strategy is built upon a fundamentally different positioning strategy. For example, it would not be prudent for GNCS to pursue a broad curriculum in the same way that it would be foolish for Apple to get into a price war with Dell. So "live and let live" is another potential strategic implication for Area C.

- **Area D:** This is nonvalue or disequity common to both competitors in the analysis. The goal here is to fix disequities if this action can contribute to your competitive advantage, reduce or eliminate attributes and benefits that customers find have little value, or potentially unearth value that has not been clearly developed or articulated to customers. Palm was the first to figure out that customers desired PDAs with a very simple set of functions, and so stripped out much of the complexity of its first generation product—to great success.

- **Area E:** Similar to Area D, except that this nonvalue or disequity is specific to our company, so there may be some very high priority fixes here. In addition, study of Area E might even emphasize the search for potential equities and unique capabilities the organization has that might be clarified and leveraged.

- **Area F:** This is the competitor's nonvalue or disequity. If chosen, the strategy of overcoming competitors' deficiencies involves making better products and services than the competition and distributing them more effectively. In addition, communications strategy can point out the problems with the competitor's offering.

- **Area G:** The white space represents areas of unmet need that neither competitor has touched. It is important to seek growth potential in unmet needs but in a structured and disciplined manner. Identify the deeper reasons underlying customer complaints and problems, and search for potential differentiating sources of new value for which we have a capability advantage.

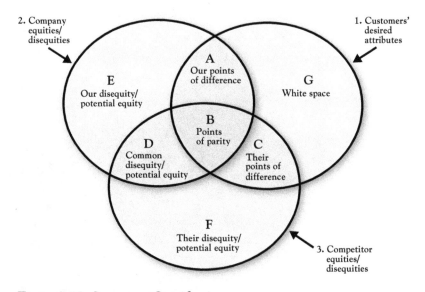

Figure 2.13. Summary: Outside view.

The inside view of the 3-Circle model captures the *back office*: the work, processes, capabilities, assets, and resources that are utilized in creating customer value. In the end, the most powerful competitive advantage emerges when your distinctive Area A, as perceived by customers, is a function of real, substantive, and distinctive capabilities and assets. Finally, the framework identifies a variety of actionable, high-impact ways in which a firm can enhance its growth prospects by building customer value that is superior to that of the competitors.

Chapters 1 and 2 have provided an overview of the framework and an introduction to the key concepts within it. Now it is time to get busy with an exploration of the core concepts in the model. Chapter 3 starts with the start—defining the context for your growth strategy analysis.

CHAPTER 3

Defining the Context

The world cannot be governed without juggling.
>   —John Selden, *The Table-Talk of John Selden*, 1892

Jugglers captivate audiences. Even juggling just three balls is an elegant and artistic act that is seemingly out of the reach of 95% of the population, given requirements of technical skill, great coordination, and focus. This is why we watch the juggler with great envy and admiration.

Yet there is a way to simplify this complex and challenging act so that everyone can do it. (Honestly, *everyone*.) Michael Gelb's brilliant discussion of juggling as a metaphor for human learning applies three key principles: (a) breaking the complex into simple pieces, (b) getting repetition on the pieces and then building them into an integrated whole, and (c) creating a language around which we can think, train, and discuss.[1]

The natural inclination of the novice juggler is to focus on *catching* the balls. Toss one, then two, then three, and try to catch. Every dropped ball is a failure and a source of frustration. Balls fly all over the place because there is no discipline in the tossing. But it takes the novice a while to realize that because he is so focused on catching the balls, he fails to see the mechanics that underlie successful juggling. The error variance caused by the many, varied throws really takes the would-be juggler away from the goal of tossing and catching the balls in an easy, controlled pattern.

Gelb's insightful method, though, brings order to this chaos by boiling the task down to its simplest components. Following it, a novice can be juggling three tennis balls comfortably in 10 to 20 minutes. We have provided an overview of the initial step in Figure 3.1 to illustrate the basic principles applied.

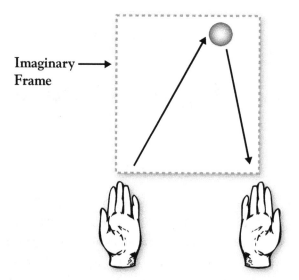

Imaginary Frame →

Figure 3.1. Juggling three balls: The initial left-hand toss.

Summary From Gelb (2003)

You begin by writing numbers on the tennis balls with a magic marker—1, 2, and 3. Put a big dot or "X" on Ball 3 to distinguish it from the other two.

Left-Hand Throw (Ball 1)

Stand facing your couch so that when you are tossing balls the couch will catch any that do not land in your hands. Holding only Ball 1 in your left hand, envision a frame floating in front of you. The frame is about the width of your shoulders and would extend vertically to a little above your eye line. Toss Ball 1 from your left hand up to the center-right part of the top of your imaginary frame, keeping your eyes looking up (don't look down at your hands). If you toss it accurately to the upper right of the frame, the ball will tend to drop straight down (see Figure 3.1). It is safe to say that your first few tosses will not be accurate. But it's not important that you catch it. Just try to throw it easily, accurately, and in a controlled way. Focus on the toss with your left hand, not the catch with your right. Pick the ball up from the couch and keep tossing. Make your throws as consistent as you can. Odds are that by the 5th or 6th throw, even though you're not trying to catch the ball in your right hand, you do (you just can't help it!). Keep practicing your left-handed throw until the ball starts dropping consistently into your right hand, keeping your eyes forward.

This fundamental principle of the accurate "left-hand toss to upper right frame" is at the center of your ability to juggle. Once the novice has experience at this basic toss, Gelb teaches how to generalize it and follow with a "right-hand toss to upper left frame" (Ball 2) and then to add Ball 3 with appropriate timing. Once Ball 3 is added, the 3-ball integrated toss is defined around the concept of a *juggulation*, an aptly named cycle that consists of three tosses and three catches. The juggler proceeds to juggling excellence by first achieving a juggulation, then practicing one juggulation at a time, then going for two juggulations one after the other, and so on.

We leave you to Gelb's books for completion of your juggling training. But there is a wonderful set of principles in this process that lay a foundation for our work on growth strategy:

- *Break down the complex into simple pieces.* Gelb's approach to teaching juggling is based on the learning principle that complex subjects can be broken down into their simpler component pieces. The first step is to envision an imaginary frame in front of you that is a little wider than your shoulders and extends from your navel to about 6 inches above your head. Gelb calls this the "juggler's box." With this frame in mind, think of a basic toss that underlies all of three-ball juggling; toss Ball 1 with your left hand to the upper right part of an imaginary frame so that it will drop down to somewhere around your right hand (see Figure 3.1). You will not be able to juggle effectively until you can reasonably perfect this basic toss.

- *Assemble the pieces into an integrated whole.* Once this basic toss is learned, it becomes easier to catch the balls. The toss is then duplicated with a second toss from the right hand, and then later integrates a third toss. The process is learn a toss, get repetition on the piece, then add another piece until the juggler has cumulatively built the full repertoire of tosses needed to complete a cycle. In sum, there is gradual integration of additional pieces until they form an elegant whole.

- *Build a common language.* Importantly, the process creates a language by which we can communicate about juggling. The terms *toss* and *catch* are quite simple but have specific meaning in this context. You know the difference between *Balls 1, 2, and 3*; we know that the *juggler's box* provides a critical reference for guiding the effort. *Juggulation*—the completion of one successful cycle of three tosses and three catches—is an important concept. Learning is facilitated by limiting your efforts to build up to learning one *juggulation* at a time and perfecting that before you move on. This term is important in communication, specifically in helping the teacher convey to the learner *what* to focus on.

The same principles are at work in our description of the 3-Circle model. What has been written on growth strategy, competitive strategy, positioning, customer analysis, competitive analysis, and company analysis can, and does, fill libraries. It is fair to describe it as chaotic, and attacking it all at once would be like trying to teach yourself to juggle by simultaneously throwing multiple balls in the air at once. Our process is designed to do exactly the same thing as Gelb's: Break down the components, integrate them back together in a way that produces effective results, and, in doing so, create a language around which to build growth strategy. The goal is to make accessible concepts that have been thought to be messy, complex, and inaccessible.

The objective in this chapter is to teach how to frame up a 3-Circle project by defining its component parts. These are the three most significant component parts that every manager juggles in growth strategy planning and execution.

Defining the Context: Overview

In developing growth strategy—as in juggling (!)—first, you need a frame that serves a purpose like the juggler's box. The difference is that the frame for growth strategy is not imaginary. Instead, it is a very real combination of the statement of a particular company unit (product, service, brand, product/service line, etc.), the customer segment, and the competitor. In fact, the generic way that we define a growth strategy project is by stating a project goal in the following way:

"My goal is to grow **COMPANY UNIT** by creating more value for **CUSTOMER SEGMENT** than **COMPETITOR** does."

This definition provides a means of building the frame for the growth strategy for a particular business unit. Some simple examples of project contexts, reflected from past projects, are the following:

- My goal is to figure out how **McDONALD'S** can grow by creating more value for **BREAKFAST CUSTOMERS** than **STARBUCKS** does.
- My goal is to figure out how **HARRAH'S CASINO** can grow by creating more value for the **HIGH NET WORTH GAMBLER** than **EMPRESS CASINO** does.
- My goal is to figure out how **ORBITZ** can grow by creating more value for **HIGH FREQUENCY TRAVELERS** than **EXPEDIA.COM** does.

This statement first requires a precise statement of each element. It puts the three dimensions of the 3-Circle project in a particular action-oriented context, focused on company growth, customer value, and a competitor. While the previous statements look fairly simple in hindsight, in reality, they are often difficult to develop. This is not because it is difficult to find things to put in the blanks. On the contrary, it is because there are often way too many things that we *could* put in the blanks!

Why a Focused Project Context Is Necessary

Stephen Johnson is a photographer wishing to build a growth strategy for his newly opened shop. Stephen's project definition states a goal of "seeking to grow *Johnson Photography* by creating more value for *customers* than *Frederick Pictures* (the local competitor)." There is a very clear problem with this statement. "Customers" is ill-defined. Once Stephen started exploring customers' value definitions and perceptions, he would find very big differences between different types of customers. For example, primary school administrators who need to choose a photographer for school pictures will have very different criteria for value (e.g., moderate quality, volume, price) and very different awareness levels than will young couples or families in the market for weddings, who would likely put more emphasis on very high quality, responsive service, and related services (e.g., video, websites), along with a greater willingness to pay. In addition, depending on the segment chosen for study, different competitors emerge. If we tried to do a growth strategy project without distinguishing between potentially different customers, we would find a confusing mass of answers because different people will define value differently and will have different competitors in mind. As a result, it is best to be as specific as possible in defining project contexts, even if that means giving up some breadth in the analysis. As we will see, the returns provided by greater depth are more than worth the depth given up.

Often, defining the context for a 3-Circle project is an excellent opportunity to look more fundamentally at your business, asking the following basic questions:

- What is the *company* "unit of analysis"?
- Who (what *customer segments*) do we serve?
- With whom do we *compete*?

The project context statement is an integrative statement that brings together these three elements. As noted later, the order of determination may well depend on the particular business problem that needs to be solved. The goal is to define the boundaries of the project in the form of a simple declarative statement that can be easily communicated to others. The best way to illustrate the subtlety—and, sometimes, frustration!—in leading to these simple statements is reflected in a series of principles. These principles provide the organizing framework for the chapter. The first principle is about chickens and eggs.

Chicken or Egg Does Not Matter

It would seem that there would be an optimal "starting point" for defining the project context statement. However, there is no single answer. If there is one natural, central defining construct in the process, it is customer decision making. This means that important issues spring from the way the customer approaches the decision—for example, what attributes, features, and benefits are important, what competitive options are considered and not considered, and so on. For the most part, the relevant dimensions of the context all spring from how the customers tend to view and make the decision. Early discussions with customers help define (a) the particular unit of analysis about which they make decisions—such as selection of one brand over another, or selection of complementary products and services at the same time, and (b) the competitive options that they consider.

That said, while an understanding of the customer segment and how customers likely choose between competitive options will somehow always be reflected in the analysis, it may not always be the first step. So what should come first in defining your initial project: the company unit, the customer segment, or the competitor? We believe that to answer this, you first need to consider your business problem. It may be that you have been observing a *segment of customers* get larger over time, representing a great opportunity, but you have been unable to build sales in that segment as quickly as you like. If so, the customer segment may be the anchor for the project. With the customer segment in mind, you then explore (a) what the relevant *company unit* (e.g., product or service line, brand, even division) is with which you can create value for this segment and (b) which *competitor(s)* you want to include in the analysis. On the other hand, maybe you have had a new competitor preying on your mind, perhaps one that is beginning to eat away at your sales. As such, a project may be motivated by a desire to develop a deeper understanding of a particular competitor. Once you anchor on a competitor, then think through the particular *company unit* with whom they compete and the most relevant *customer segment* you both serve. Finally, you may start with the *company unit*—once defined—for example, perhaps you have carried around the broader problem of how to grow the business unit. This one is broader by definition, in that it could conceivably involve different segments and competitors, so may require a bit more search and analysis in its development.

Without a particular business problem in mind, we will start with the company unit of analysis, noting that there is a common thread across all three areas to help define the basic dimensions of the project—that common thread is *customer choice.*

Define the Company Unit of Analysis So It Is Actionable

This is usually straightforward, so we will spend little time here. If the company is small and interacts with customers with a single product, it may be that the unit of analysis is just the company itself. Alternatively, the project may be organized around a particular product line. Consider the following project context statement from Medline, an Illinois-based manufacturer of hospital clothing and supplies: "How Medline can grow *our fashion scrubs business* by creating more value for hospital employees in a color by discipline program than a local scrub store?" In this case, the company unit is a newer line of scrubs that is targeted to hospitals who have adopted a color-by-discipline program in which the hospital employees role can be identified by the color they wear. This project was undertaken by the product manager responsible for the line who was exploring the potential for an online retail store presence.

The key criterion in defining context will almost always be a function of customer choice. There are many dimensions on which the company unit can be defined. It could be defined by an individual brand or an umbrella brand (covering multiple brands). It could be defined by an individual product or service or by a line of products or services. It is less likely to be a broad business unit, though, because what is critical is that the unit of analysis be some unit around which we can define customer choice; that is, the company unit must be the subject of choice. In short, *we need to define the company as a unit of analysis where the dimensions of value on which customers compare our offering to competitors' can be identified.* As an example, we can define the reasons why customers might choose between Medline's online store and a local bricks-and-mortar retail store; such factors would include time savings, ability to control shopping time frame, pricing, ability to try on goods, ability to physically inspect the products, immediacy of purchase, and so on. In contrast, it would be difficult to frame a project around Medline's multidivision product line against that of a similar competitor. Why? Because people do not evaluate whether to choose one Medline division over another (or even over competitors). In contrast, evaluating a narrower product line or category provides a concrete starting point for a project. The general comparison of Dell versus Apple for the purposes of developing growth strategy is relevant only within particular product or service lines. Otherwise, it would be a general analysis of brand meaning, which, while useful for understanding brand equity, falls short of useful growth strategy development for particular areas of the firm.

Think About Customer Segments

Most companies (whether they know it or not) serve multiple customer segments. That is, different customers purchase the company's products or services for different reasons. If we can recognize and understand those different reasons, it is possible to change our marketing mix, custom-tailoring it to different segments to generate a better share of each segment's sales than if we had a "one size fits all" offering. A hypothetical example is presented in Figure 3.2, illustrating how a bottled-water company might substantially increase its total contribution by recognizing that there are different segments of consumers. Treating all consumers the same (with a single product, i.e., the "undifferentiated" case), the company offers one product at a price of $1.00 and a margin of $0.50. However, through a little research, the company learns that different customers have different purchase motivations. It turns out that 70% of the market is price driven, and enjoys paying $1.00 for the current product. The other 30%, however, is concerned with health. The latter segment would like a product that is vitamin-fortified, and is willing to pay more for it. The calculations appear in the Appendix to this chapter, but the conclusion is that the firm's total contribution increases from $75 previously (selling just the single product) to $115 when two products are offered. This is because the healthy segment will buy more of a product that better meets their needs, and their willingness to pay $1.50 provides a higher margin on each bottle sold (see the "differentiated" scenario on the right in Figure 3.2). In sum, there is an economic logic to market segmentation—firms engage in the practice because it increases profitability.

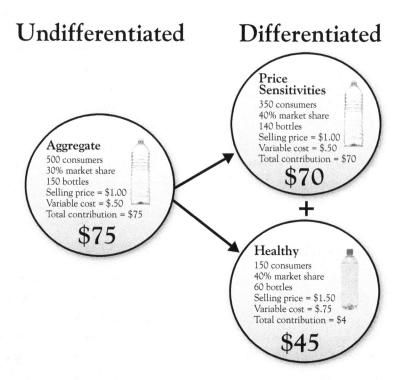

Undifferentiated   # Differentiated

Price Sensitivities
350 consumers
40% market share
140 bottles
Selling price = $1.00
Variable cost = $.50
Total contribution = $70

$70

Aggregate
500 consumers
30% market share
150 bottles
Selling price = $1.00
Variable cost = $.50
Total contribution = $75

$75

+

Healthy
150 consumers
40% market share
60 bottles
Selling price = $1.50
Variable cost = $.75
Total contribution = $4

$45

Figure 3.2. Increased profitability potential for differentiating between market segments.

There are hundreds of textbooks and trade books that provide insight into "how" markets can be segmented. There are many different ways to segment the market, but there is a basic logic that is common across approaches:[2]

- Identify different types of benefits that customers seek from your product
- Group customers together based on the benefits they seek
- Use other descriptors to describe the segments—for example, demographics like age, income, firm size, and location

Segmentation Is About Reasons

An important way to think about market segments is to consider how different people might decide to buy a product or service for different reasons. Some people buy for price alone, for example. In contrast, others are willing to pay a high price for convenience.

The following exercise can be used to explore the reasons for customer choice in the market you are looking to study. Let us take the example of gasoline service stations. What segments might exist in this market? One way of addressing this would be to speak with those who have fairly extensive experience in the market (e.g., service station operators, executives). While their knowledge of the market may not be perfect—and they will have varying opinions—they will have insights that will help you move forward. In addition, you might have conversations with 5 to 10 customers—even just people you know—as almost all consumers have experience in this service category. But the goal of these discussions is to identify the general needs (e.g., the reasons why people need the service in the first place) and then the reasons why a customer chooses one service station over another. This exercise can be framed as a simple question: why did you choose service station A over service station B?[3] Let us say the reasons that emerge in this analysis include the following:

- Prices good; saves me money
- Fast service; saves me time
- Needed milk; they have a big product assortment
- I know and like the people there; relationship
- Convenient location on my way to work; close to my house
- Very neat; well maintained

Now, looking at these reasons, two things become clear: (a) different people are likely to emphasize different reasons for choosing a service station (*people segments*), and (b) there are likely to be times when the same person might make a choice for different reasons (*situation segments*). People segments are easiest to think about, as we group different people into reason-based segments. So, for example, consider Table 3.1 in which—based on preliminary research and conversations with customers—we identify three segments that place different weights on the reasons we listed previously.

The segments are largely defined by different needs. The first segment tends to seek low gas prices first and foremost, and other concerns are

Table 3.1. Describing Customer Segments for Service Stations

	Segment descriptions		
	Price driven: always searching for the lowest price in the market	**On-the-go snackers:** frequent stops for snacks and food items in addition to gas	**Loyalists:** very loyal to a particular service station; considered a "regular"
	How important is each reason to each segment? (L = low importance, M = moderate, H = high)		
• Prices good/saves me money	H	M	L
• Fast service/saves me time	M	H	H
• Needed milk/they have a big product assortment	L	H	M
• I know and like the people there/relationship	M	M	H
• Convenient location on my way to work	M	L	M
• Close to my house	L	L	M
• Very neat, well maintained	L	M	H

secondary. The second segment seeks food product assortment and variety. The third segment is happy to pay higher prices because they value consistently patronizing a service station where expectations are regularly met and there is value in the relationship built with the staff. This is the basis for market segmentation: Different people choose certain products for different reasons.

Defining the Project With a Segment Focus

The point of exploring customer segments in your market is that, most of the time, it is best to keep a project focused on one segment. The clearer a picture you have of the particular customers you are seeking to grow business with, the deeper and more insightful your project will be. For example, Harley-Davidson management could define a project as having the goal of "growing sales by creating more value for *heavy weight motorcycle riders* than does Honda." The challenge with this customer definition is that it is very broad, encompassing many different types of customers who purchase motorcycles for very different reasons. Envisioning growth among customers requires a very close look at who they are and "why they buy." Based on research summarized in Winer,[5] there are, in fact, at least six different customer segments of Harley purchasers, ranging from "tour gliders" (about 14% of Harley purchasers) to the much larger "dream rider" segment, which accounts for 40% of Harley's market. The tour gliders use their bikes for long trips for recreation and relaxation, tend to buy more expensive bikes, and spend twice as much on accessories as the dream riders, who tend to ride many fewer miles—mostly local—and appear to be "outlaw wannabes." If a growth strategy project mixed these two segments, it would be difficult to sort out value—the tour gliders seek bike comfort for long trips, while the dream riders seek shine and glitz in a less expensive bike that makes them a "hog." The individual preferences of each segment would be blurred if we tried to do a project that lumped them together. In addition, these different segments may each have different competitive brands in mind when they choose their motorcycles. That leads us to the next principle.

Choose Competitor That Are Relevant to Target Customers

There are a variety of strategic considerations in selecting a competitor or competitors for your growth strategy project. But two general rules capture the most important issues:

1. Identify competitors that your target customer gives serious consideration to when choosing a product or service in this category.
2. Out of that set, select a competitor that is strategically relevant to you—that is, one that currently affects your business or will affect it in the future in terms of market share and profit potential.

Identifying the competitors that your customer considers is actually pretty straightforward—it just takes a few conversations with customers, asking the question, "When you thought about buying a product or service in this category, what were all the options you considered?" But you will also need to keep in mind a broad field of vision for identifying your competitors. You may think of your competitor as the firm that is most like you or that is your biggest potential threat in terms of market share and profitability. Your customer may have other ideas. A systematic way to think about potential competitors is captured in Figure 3.3, which depicts concentric circles representing competition at different levels. If our target brand for assessment is Diet Coke, for example, we can argue that its closest direct "form" competitor is Diet Pepsi—the two are of the same exact product form, and each is a national brand. Yet we know that Diet Coke competes at other levels with other brands and options. At the product category level, there are many other soda products that the consumer might consider, including national, regional, and local brands. At an even broader level, it is conceivable that, at times, a consumer may choose between having a Diet Coke and a cup of coffee (or another beverage that is not soda). Finally, the budget level of competition may include all things that might compete for that $1.50 spent on a Diet Coke. It might be a bag of potato chips or pretzels, a comic book, or a candy bar.

This brings us to the point concerning selecting competitors based on strategic relevance. The general guidance here assumes that strategic relevance relates to degree of current or future impact of a competitor. This might take one of several forms: (a) selecting a large, fierce competitor,

Every product or service has both direct and indirect competition. These competitors can be identified as product form, product category, generic, and budget competition.

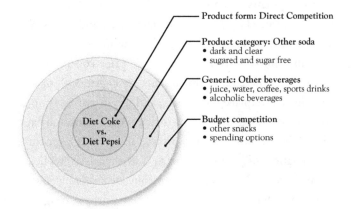

Figure 3.3. Levels of competition.

(b) selecting a competitor who has been gradually creeping up, or (c) selecting a competitor out on the horizon who might have an interest in the market. Again, your decision here should be based on current strategic priorities—from what type of analysis do you stand to gain the most? Which competitor (large current threat, future threat, distant future threat on the horizon) represents the most relevant analysis for you today?

Multiple Customer Segments, Multiple Competitors

There will no doubt be multiple customer segments that you will identify as important, as well as multiple competitors. As we noted earlier in the chapter, though, it is important that any given project have a focus on one of each. As an example, Sarah is a brand manager with Procter & Gamble, and she is considering a 3-Circle project in which she is exploring the goal of "growing the Pampers brand by creating more value for customer segment than competitor."

In truth, there are many interesting combinations of customer segments and competitors that Pampers might study here. The first basic

distinction in customer segments might be between retailers and consumers. If Sarah chose retailers—in an effort to improve value in the
interest of securing valuable shelf space in stores—there in fact would
be subsegments to consider: traditional high-low grocery stores, everyday low-price chains, mass merchandisers, and so on. Within consumer
segments, there are many ways that the market might be segmented: by
benefits (time-constrained moms vs. price-constrained moms), geogra-
phy (cold climate vs. warm climate; see Figure 3.4), or other demographics. The marketplace is complex, and it is important not to gloss over that
complexity. What this means is that we are almost always best served by
identifying an initial project around the market segment and competitor
combination of greatest interest, and then later replicating it on other
combinations. There are two reasons why this narrow starting point is
important. First, as we will see, one gets deeper insight when the analysis is focused on a particular customer segment and competitor combination than if customer segments and competitors are "aggregated." To

Figure 3.4. Pampers cold climate diaper ad.

illustrate, consider the answers we get from customers on the question, "Overall, does Pampers meet, exceed, or fall below your expectations on the following dimensions: fair price, readily available at the store, and easy to change the baby?" Answers on the three dimensions may differ significantly for different consumer segments. If we lumped all segments together, we would likely be mixing consumers with quite different beliefs and importance ratings. Note the same argument holds if our analysis is to focus on *retailers* as customers. Buyers and other decision makers within conventional grocery stores will likely place very different levels of importance and beliefs on product attributes than buyers from mass merchandisers.

So to the extent you can, analyze market segments separately. In fact, if you have the resources to conduct analysis on different customer-segment-competitor combinations, it provides for a very powerful comparison and contrast of such analyses. Finding commonalities between them—say, common dimensions of Area A—would reflect strong evidence of brand equity. The lack of such commonalities would indicate concerns about brand equity and the bases of customer choice.

Stay Open to Broader Applications

The most frequent application of the 3-Circle model has been in competitive market situations in which the firm is seeking to grow its business for particular customer segments in the face of competition. However, application is limited only by our ability to envision the potential choice of anyone who we might define as a "customer." As a result, the framework can be broadly applied to almost any leadership situation. For example, the human resources department has internal customers who choose between its services and outside headhunters. The marketing research department has internal customers who choose between its services and going ahead on a decision without research. We have frontline employees who choose whether to buy in to a new operating process or not. We have employees who choose whether to commit to a new business vision or not. The more we can understand and respect the value that each of these parties seeks and is driven by in these decisions, the more likely it is we can figure out how to create and substantively build that value.

As an illustration, consider a vice president or general manager tasked with determining whether or not we even need the 3-person market research department that the organization has had for 20 years. When economic times are challenging, the goal should not simply be to slash. The goal should be to determine where we can do the needed work both more effectively and efficiently. This requires understanding the value created by the market research department for its customers (and, down the chain, the perspective of those customers on how the group contributes to the value created for the firm's end customers). A project context could be usefully stated as follows: "My goal is to determine whether outsourcing market research provides superior value for internal research users than does the current market research department."

We might define internal research users more specifically (e.g., new product development teams or teams involved in mergers and acquisitions), as again, needs will vary depending on the customer. However, what is important here is that this analysis digs more deeply into the value sought by the research users in the organization rather than simply seeking to find justification for budget dollars. We will find that the search for, and understanding of, that value provides a basis for making decisions that will enhance the organization's profitability in the longer term by *better aligning resources with the firm's real needs.*

Chapter Summary: A Matter of Choice

Life is fundamentally about choices, and people make many different kinds of choices in the marketplace. We choose one competitive brand over another. We choose to work for one firm and not another firm. We choose to buy in to management's new process initiative or stick with the old way. At the core, the goal of leadership in the marketplace and in organizations is to create conditions to give a high probability to choices *coming our way.* The most effective way of accomplishing this is to uncover, deeply understand, and respect the value that people seek in these choices. Surprisingly, we rarely take the time to do this. So those who do take the time enjoy a *big* advantage over those who do not.

Defining the context in a 3-Circle project is critical, as it helps managers or analysts really get their hands around the choices being made, why such choices are made, and where the growth opportunities exist. The more clearly and precisely the decision context is defined, the deeper the insights, the stronger the analysis, and further—paradoxically—the more likely the insights will generalize to other contexts. The real value of a context well defined is the ability to really deeply explore the value sought by the customer.

The key principles of context definition include:

- Clearly define the company "unit" under study—with what unit are you creating value (a department, a product or service line, you or yourself, a service department, etc.)?
- Clearly define the customer segment who you would like to choose your offering. The key is to understand the value this segment seeks. Segment "selection" presumes that we already know how the market is segmented; in fact, you may need a segmentation exercise before you can select.
- Choose a competitor who is a viable object of choice for the customer.
- Remember that—even though an apparent "narrow" context may seem overly restrictive—the resulting depth of analysis more than compensates for the limited breadth. We can apply the analysis to other customer segments and competitors later.

Appendix: The Economics of Market Segmentation

Imagine that a company sells bottled water in a market of 500 customers, each of whom consumes one bottle during a given period of time (e.g., a day, every 2 days; the particular period is not relevant). The company sells its water for $1.00. Its variable cost is $0.50 and it has a 30% share of the market. That means it sells 150 bottles every period (500 × 30%) and earns a $75 contribution (150 bottles times a unit margin of $0.50; see Figure 3.2, undifferentiated section on left).

The company keeps its eyes and ears open, however, and discovers that there are some consumers who enjoy bottled water and also believe that water might be a vehicle through which to obtain additional vitamins. In short, they represent a growing segment interested in health and in the impact of the products they consume on their well-being. Additional research identifies that of the 500 folks in the market, the health-driven segment now totals 150 people! These folks would get a lot of value out of a bottled water product that is vitamin-fortified.

Your product development folks figure out how to add vitamins for an extra $0.25 per bottle, raising your variable costs to $0.75. When this product enters the market, it reveals more about how the market has been (unbeknownst to you) segmented all along—see the right-hand portion of Figure 3.2 labeled "differentiated." The top circle reveals the fact that 70% of the market is actually price sensitive and enjoys the existing product at the low price of $1.00. It turns out that you have about a 40% share of this segment, so these folks accounted for 140 of the 150 bottles you were selling when you only had one undifferentiated product on the market. If we keep that product on the market and add a new product to appeal to the healthy segment, we increase our total contribution from $75 to $115! How does this happen? Well, we find that—if we have been on target in our new product development—the healthy segment is much more likely to purchase the vitamin-fortified product, even though it costs 50% more than our standard product. In fact, we get a 40% share of the healthy market, selling at a unit margin of $0.75, producing a total contribution of $45. Adding this to the $70 we earn from the price-sensitive market, we have increased total contribution from $75 to $115 by (a) understanding that there are segments in the marketplace, and (b) effectively targeting them.[6]

CHAPTER 4

The Meaning of Value

In August 2008, CEO Mike Lenahan was finding growth to be challenging for his firm Resource Recovery Corporation (RRC). RRC is a small competitor in the recycling industry, geographically constrained with a pool of about 30 customers, all of whom are foundries. Foundries use tons of sand weekly for moldings and then need to dispose of it. RRC was created in the interest of reducing disposal cost and identifying reuses of the spent sand and other materials. The company had very close relationships with this customer base, in part because in 1991, about 15 of these 30 foundries had actually banded together to form RRC, as a low-cost competitive alternative to the large recycling firms, including Waste Management. These large competitors had more recently constrained RRC's growth.

As part of a 3-Circle project, Mike's executive team undertook interviews with customers to learn more about how they valued their service versus the service of competitors. Issues of cost levels, aspects of the firm's recycling methods, speed of service, reliability, and size of the company all came up in the discussions with customers. Many of the customer assessments were positive on these dimensions. When it came to size of the company, RRC executives felt that their small size was a significant advantage to them in the eyes of the customer. Mike and his team believed that small meant fast on the feet and responsive, a major advantage over very large competitors slowed down by corporate hierarchy. However, when they explored the deeper meaning of "firm size" to customers, they were stunned. Instead of seeing RRC's firm size as a strength, customers saw it as a *weakness*. When Mike and his team dug into this assessment, they found customers to be concerned about the *long-term viability* of a small firm in an industry in which four large competitors have over half of the market share. In other words, the sentiment they heard was "we know you're good and we love your cost model, but we don't know if you are going to be around in five years."

RRC quickly responded to these concerns and, within a month, increased its sales at a level that represented 10% of the company's annual sales. This was accomplished by conducting a strategic review of all the capabilities, resources, and assets the firm had access to that signaled longer-term stability. They had recently firmed up a variety of resource commitments and external partnerships and had asset investments and customer relationships that reflected a clear external commitment to the firm into the future. The RRC team then developed a sales strategy that focused customers' attention on the strength of these resource commit-ments and relationships, and returned to these customers. On top of an already compelling cost model, this allowed the team to land an account that had been sitting on the fence for some time, and provided a robust piece of revenue that has helped stabilize the firm in more recent reces-sionary times.

Mike Lenahan runs a smart company that is *very* close to its custom-ers. Yet in these relationships—and unbeknownst to RRC—customers' persistent belief that "small equals unstable" had existed for some time, limiting their sales growth. Is it uncommon for executives to feel confi-dent that they know customers but to then get blindsided by unexpected customer assessments? In 3-Circle projects with over 200 executives, we have found the majority indicating surprise at the insights obtained. Most managers initially believe that they have a reasonable, intuitive under-standing of the value customers seek. Yet with deeper discussions with customers, they very frequently discover insights that materially improve growth strategies.

But can we get a broader sense of the payoffs from deeper under-standing of customer value? In an important research study that pro-vides the foundation for his Momentum Effect model of growth, Jean-Claude Larreche of INSEAD examined the financial results for 367 of the largest worldwide companies for the 20-year period from 1985 through 2004. Some of the most interesting discoveries from the research focused upon the 119 leading consumer goods firms.[1] Larreche sorted these consumer firms into three groups: those firms that increased, those that decreased, and those that held constant advertising expenditures over that time period (where advertising spending was measured by the advertising-to-sales ratio, or A/S). Consistent with a traditional view, more intensive advertising was found to produce positive financial results, as measured by improvement of firm value. The group that increased its A/S ratio over time (labeled *pushers* by Larreche) experienced improvement in market capitalization that was 28% higher than the firms who held their A/S ratios roughly constant (labeled *plodders*). Improvement in market capitalization over time for the pushers matched the average change in the Dow Jones index for the same time period, indicating that "marketing as pushing" is a reasonably successful strategy. Figure 4.1 shows the results for these two groups as the first two bars, indicating that increasing advertising intensity leads to greater stock market value.

However, note that there is a third group that Larreche identified: the firms that actually *reduced* their advertising spending over time. Based on the apparent positive effect of greater advertising intensity for pushers, we might expect that this third group would significantly underperform over

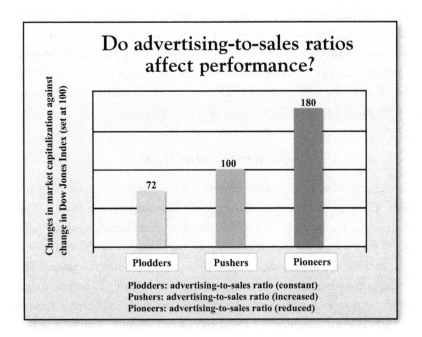

Figure 4.1. Stock market performance of plodders, pushers, and pioneers.

Source: Adapted from "Momentum Strategy for Efficient Growth: When the Sumo Meets the Surfer," by J-C. Larreche, 2008, *International Commerce Review*, 8, 22–34.

time. Yet they not only beat the Plodders by 108%, they also substantially outperformed the *pushers* (by 80%)! This stunning result has a simple interpretation. It is *not* that these firms found advertising ineffective, reduced it, and subsequently increased performance. Instead, it is that there is another element of strategy to consider: the excellence of their products and services. This third group—labeled the *pioneers*—includes firms that design products and services with such *compelling and unique value* that they create their own sales momentum. In short, demand for these firms' products and services is less a function of advertising and communications and more a function of how well they deliver the value that customers seek. In essence, these firms allow their actual offerings to do the talking.

So where do these more compelling offerings come from? Whether the firm is Apple, Starbucks, Southwest Airlines, FedEx, or Mike Lenahan's Resource Recovery Corporation, the compelling offerings come from a deeper understanding of *customer value* than competitors have. This chapter defines and explores customer value. We first consider the fundamental dimensions of customer value and then consider how studying these dimensions can help in understanding competitive dynamics and growth strategy. We further consider that there are important growth opportunities in thinking more broadly and deeply about customer value than competitors do. The last section of the chapter overviews an approach to engaging the study of customer value.

Customer Value Basics

Sometimes, customers' choices are difficult for a firm to understand. Consider Chris, a consumer evaluating two brands of aspirin side-by-side. One brand, the national brand, costs $5.99. The other brand, a store brand, costs $3.19 for a package that contains more than twice the quantity in the national brand's package. Chris winces when she sees the price difference, as she is managing her household under an end-of-the-month budget constraint, so even a couple of dollars really matter. In addition, Chris has a high degree of confidence—based on research evidence and the reported conclusions of the U.S. Food and Drug Administration (FDA)—that one unit of the generic brand provides essentially the same performance and benefits as one unit of the national brand. Yet, after brief consideration, Chris grabs the national brand and puts it in her shopping cart.

Observing such a decision would be extremely disheartening to two people: (a) a classical economist, and (b) the category manager for the retailer who wishes to build their store brands. The decision would not make sense to the economist, who assumes that consumers are utility maximizing. The economist knows that, given full knowledge of the brands, Chris should choose the best value for the money. Similarly, the store category manager might be equally disappointed over Chris's choice, as the manager is seeking to build the private label brand's sales performance.

But Chris's decision makes sense when one considers the reality that she sees. She is buying the aspirin for her husband, who was just advised by his doctor after a check-up to take one aspirin a day for circulation. This decision is linked to a very important concern for her: the health and safety of her spouse, which motivates her to manage risk. Further, the national brand was always in the medicine cabinet at her home when she was a little girl. She has a deep and abiding trust in the brand, as her mother was always a loyal purchaser. Although dressed in packaging with similar colors and design, the store's private label brand, positioned right next to the popular national brand, has plainer and less informative packaging. Yet Chris remembers reading an FDA conclusion that generics can be expected to produce the same benefits as the brand-name equivalent provided they have gone through the same approval process. So with a very high level of confidence, she assumes these two brands are very similar in the basic benefits they deliver.

In the end, though, this is not a decision where she wants to take the chance that the private label manufacturer did not "go through the approval process." This will be a product her husband will be taking regularly, for a long period of time, to keep him healthy. In addition, although her husband has never had a stomach problem from using aspirin, she notes that the national brand has a coating, which may help in everyday consumption, just in case. For a brand with which she is more assured, Chris is happy to pay $2.80 more for a package containing less than half the number of aspirin tablets. From different perspectives, this decision may not make sense to people, yet it makes complete sense to Chris.

Customer Value: Some Basic Concepts

As we have discussed, a common representation of customer choice is to summarize key reasons for purchase as *benefits* or *costs*, and to suggest that the customer makes an overall evaluation of each choice option, comparing these concepts.[2] The benefits represent what the customer *gets* from the purchase. This "get" can be broken down into component parts, often identified as attributes. Recall that in chapter 2, we defined attribute to *be an inherent characteristic or a quality of some object.* In Chris's decision, she considered attributes such as *effectiveness, package size, familiarity* with the brand, and whether the aspirin is *easy on the stomach.* What is the "give"? This is Chris's perceptions of the costs of the purchase, represented most predominantly by the *price* in this case. Two issues briefly bear further discussion.

First, somehow, Chris obviously combines this information to come to a choice. We know that she considered price and package size trade-offs, for example, and further integrated her trust in the brand. There is no one particular method by which customers choose—some people may be completely price driven (i.e., "always choose the lowest price"), while others may be totally driven by a perceived benefit (e.g., "always choose the most effective").[3] For our purposes in this book, we will get enough information in knowing that (a) customers make choices, (b) those choices involve evaluating different options on particular attributes, and (c) those attributes vary in importance.

The second point is to distinguish between *attributes* and *benefits*, but then to suggest that we will often refer to them in the same breath. While an attribute is an inherent quality or characteristic of a product or service, a *benefit* is a result or outcome associated with consuming that product or service. So while effectiveness (measured by amount of pain killer in the aspirin) could be considered a feature or attribute of aspirin, the associated benefit of consuming the aspirin is that "I feel better quickly." Alternatively, the benefit attached to a larger package size is that "I don't have to go to the store as often." Very often, measurement of customer beliefs is made at the attribute level because attributes are concrete and easy to envision. We will soon see that the consumer's translation of attributes to benefits (and then even deeper values) becomes critically important for creating distinctive value around which growth strategy can be built. Before we get there, though, let us consider attributes as dimensions of value in more depth.

Attributes and Competition: Six Lessons

In the preceding analysis, the attribute is the key unit of analysis—it might be thought of as the DNA of customer choice. Let us first consider some basic principles underlying the evolution of competition in a given market. In his book *Strategic Marketing Management: A Means-End Approach*,[4] Mark Parry provides an excellent illustration of the principles described here in his analysis of a seemingly simple product category—toothpaste. Beginning with Pepsodent in the 1920s, and its appeal to white teeth and attractiveness, and carrying through to developments of fluoride, health, and good parenting (e.g., Crest, in 1956), packaging (e.g., first pump in 1984 by a brand called Check-Up), and baking soda (Arm & Hammer, in 1986) as examples, Parry's work illustrates the story of competitive dynamics in the market as a story of attributes and benefits. This historical review provides a helpful context in which to highlight the following key principles regarding customer-value dynamics and competition.[5]

Lesson 1: *Every choice option—particularly products and services in the marketplace—can be broken down into attributes and benefits.* Figure 4.2 is a picture of a contemporary package of Crest toothpaste. How many attributes and benefits are reflected on the label? A quick count shows at least seven—tartar control, whitening, with Scope, minty fresh, liquid gel, fluoride anticavity, and strengthens enamel. Note that the attributes are presented as factual statements of product features (e.g., "contains fluoride"), while benefits reflect outcomes of using the product (e.g., "strengthens enamel").

Lesson 2: *Certain attributes and benefits are required just to be in the game.* Some attributes and benefits in a category are "stakes of the game"— your brand needs to have them just to play. So competing automobile manufacturers make vehicles with four wheels and a steel or aluminum chassis that run (largely) on gasoline and get people from point A to point B. These attributes represent the "core" product. For toothpaste, the core product is simply having an agent of some form (the choices now include paste, liquid, or gel) designed to clean teeth and made available in easy-to-use packaging, conveniently distributed in high-frequency locations.

Lesson 3: *Other attributes and benefits provide differentiation.* A fundamental law of the marketplace, however, is that competitors seek growth

Figure 4.2. How many attributes?

by differentiation. That is, in order to motivate and incentivize customer choice of their brand, the firm seeks to make it different from the competition in a way that is important to customers. So, for example, Crest was the first to introduce fluoride as an ingredient (an attribute) in 1955. That introduction created the modern era of competition in the toothpaste market. In the intervening 40 years, the innovation and product development in this category has been fast and furious.

Lesson 4: *Once-differentiating attributes eventually become common, competition evolves around the ebb and flow of new attributes and benefits, which accumulate over time.* Parry follows the evolution of the toothpaste product category, beginning with initial value-added attributes around taste, whitening, and social benefits. But Crest's introduction of fluoride protection and subsequent endorsement from the American Dental Association in 1960 turned the market on its head. This created a new subcategory called "therapeutic," which gained 14.5% of the market by 1960 and 54.7% by 1965.[6] Today, however, we find that nearly all toothpaste brands have fluoride. In other words, fluoride has gone from being a differentiating attribute for Crest to being a must-have. (This is an idea explored in more detail in the next chapter.) But there is a critical point here in understanding the dynamics of competition. The tendency to seek differentiation builds on itself. Firms produce a constant stream of new ideas when the power of the last idea to distinguish the brand has "worn out." This leads to a situation in which attributes are added over time, each with an eye toward seeking a differential advantage for the brand and each urgent when competitors have copied the last new feature. Table 4.1 illustrates, for the toothpaste category, how those value-adding features or benefits *accumulate.* The product becomes much more complex than it was at the start and enormous variety ensues. The point here is that there may in fact be growth opportunity in understanding this accumulation—in part because some attributes that were once differentiators may in fact become expendable over time!

Lesson 5: *While attributes reflect features, ingredients, or characteristics of a choice option, benefits represent the consequences or outcomes of using that choice option.* One of the most often-repeated phrases in the

Table 4.1. Benefits From Toothpaste

	Output benefits	**Process benefits**
Functional benefits	• Removes plaque • Helps prevent tartar formation • Whitens teeth • Helps prevent tooth decay • Helps prevent gum disease • Protects tooth enamel • Healthy teeth • Good health • Fresh breath	• Easy dispensing • Less cleaning • Save time • Less packing waste • Brush longer
Experiential benefits	• A pretty smile • Teeth feel clean	• Pleasant taste • No hand pain • Feels like it is working
Financial benefits	• Save money on dentist bills	• Pay less for toothpaste • Less toothpaste waste
Psychosocial benefits	• Attractiveness	• Less irritation • Fun • Environmentally responsible • Pleasant memories

Source: Adapted from *Strategic marketing management: A means-end approach*, by M. Parry, 2002, p. 36, Exhibit 2.8, New York, NY: McGraw-Hill.

discipline of marketing is that "people buy benefits, not attributes." This is a significant point, one often lost in practice. Chris Wirthwein, an ad agency CEO, describes his recent desire to indulge a childhood passion and purchase a telescope to "explore the universe again." When he began shopping, Wirthwein had a general idea about the benefits he sought but was essentially a novice beginning at square one. What he found were manufacturers' websites that were very thorough at explaining the detailed technical features of their telescopes but extremely poor in making sense of them for potential buyers:

> Everyone talked over my head. On every website I visited, the copy seemed to have been written not for humans but for some race of unemotional alien beings. I was promised diffraction-limited Schmidt-Newtonians, achromatic refraction, and German-type equatorial mounting. I was enticed with enhanced aluminum coatings and large aperture Dobsonians . . . [the dealers' websites] were more muddled and confusing than the manufacturers' sites.[7]

In fact, there is a certain cause and effect for customers in choice and consumption behavior. We eat and that satiates our hunger. We drink and that satisfies our thirst. We look into a telescope and experience the thrill of exploring the stars. So when we buy, we do our best to estimate whether the attributes of the offering will get us to the outcomes we seek. The reason fluoride became such an important attribute for Crest to add was that it so clearly linked to higher-order, significant personal benefit for consumers (i.e., fluoride $\rightarrow$ cavity prevention $\rightarrow$ good health). As customers, we tend to think in terms of outcomes from using the product or service. In contrast, firms tend to think in terms of the features of the products or services that they have spent so much time developing, often without fully thinking through whether the product or service will do the job the customer would like to get done.

A key to building growth strategy is to think broadly and think deeply. *Thinking broadly* means breaking outside of a current view of your product or service just in terms of price, quality, and service. Your product or service, and the way you interact with customers, produces all sorts of outcomes or benefits for them, with many dimensions. It is important to put meaning on those benefits. *Thinking deeply* means recognizing that there are deeper values or problems that drive customers' decision making. Understanding this can literally be the difference between big success or failure of a new product. The idea of thinking broadly means to stop for a moment and consider the different potential dimensions on which customers may get value from your firm and your offering. So what are the *types of benefits* that customers might experience in purchasing and consuming products or services? As outlined here, there are many more than you may realize.

- *Functional: Does the product or service provide some basic outcome or consequence that the customer values?* This is truly the direct cause-effect type of instrumental benefit—for example, I drink a Red Bull, I feel energized (I have wiiings!). What are the outcomes your customers seek from consuming your product or service? Does your offering provide this value reliably and consistently?
- *Place: Is there value for the customer in the convenience and accessibility of location in acquiring this brand?* This is about meeting customer needs regarding lot size, market decentralization, waiting time for orders, product variety, and service backup. Although cutting back on locations more recently, Starbucks has certainly gained enormous value in ubiquity over time, as have their customers. Procter & Gamble developed a distribution strategy aimed at reaching tens of thousands of small, high-frequency stores in areas outside larger Mexican cities that accounted for $16 billion in sales annually.[8]
- *Financial: Are there financial benefits associated with your offering?* To some degree, this is associated with the firms that are positioned as low-cost leaders—such as Dell, McDonald's, and Southwest Airlines. However, there is a literature in economics and marketing that identifies and explores a unique impact of the feeling of a "good deal."[9]
- *Information: Does the customer feel "informed" in consuming its products or services?* There is enormous potential competitive advantage here in building more clarity into products and services. An example is Exempla Healthcare Systems, which was a

pioneer in the publication of internal quality and performance, including mortality data for various conditions and procedures.

- *Time: Does the consumer perceive value in the speed of service and general timesaving in consuming this brand?* Part of the issue here is saving time, which is a natural benefit in terms of "time for other things." However, there are more subtle dimensions. For example, research has found that providing an explanation of waiting time gave consumers greater satisfaction with the experience because it provides a greater sense of *control*.[10]

- *Relationship: Does the customer feel connected to this brand, past experiences, and employees?* This is a close cousin to the *symbolic* factor still to be discussed. Apple is a good example of a brand with which customers feel a strong resonance and personal connection.

- *Experiential: Does the customer get particular enjoyment or satisfaction out of the consumption experience?* Disney's value is built around experience, as are Starbucks stores, through the music and ambience. But interestingly, almost all product and service consumption has some experiential dimensions, including Wal-Mart (Ever get greeted at the front door with a nice "hello" from a smiling senior citizen?).

- *Symbolic: Is the consumer proud to wear this brand on his or her sleeve?* Rolex watches, Pierre Cardin clothing, and automobile brands like Lexus, Mercedes, and BMW are all quite visible representations of personal value for customers. The values may be related to success or achievement, or they may be related to affiliation with other reference people or groups. The same holds in business-to-business markets. For many years, IBM was the dominant supplier of PCs in the workplace: It was risky for corporate buyers *not* to buy the IBM brand. IBM was a symbol of success and smart, low-risk purchasing behavior within the firm.

- *Psychosocial: Does the consumer relate to other people through consuming our product?* Product or service consumption experiences at times create benefits for us in how we relate to others. So purchasing those tickets for the NBA game not only leads to personal enjoyment but also to a chance to impress a client.

Table 4.1—which also organizes consumer benefits around several of the benefit categories mentioned previously—illustrates a psychosocial benefit through "attractiveness to others." That is, one benefit of using a particular brand of toothpaste may be that your fresh breath and white teeth will help in making a positive impression on others.

Lesson 6: *Attributes are only important because they produce outcomes relevant to the customer's values.* The story behind DuPont's success with Teflon illustrates this point. Teflon was derived from a solid called polytetrafluoroethylene (PTFE) discovered in 1938, one of the most slippery materials in existence. A French engineer named Marc Gregoire later discovered how to bond the material to aluminum. Teflon-coated cookware became available in the United States in the 1960s. But DuPont's early efforts to promote this new product around the functional benefit of "fat-free cooking" produced poor results. It was not until the product was repositioned around a different functional benefit, "fast clean up," that sales took off. Why? Interestingly, it is the same attribute (Teflon coating) and the same benefit (stuff will not stick to it) in either case. Yet the real tale is told by customers' deeper values and benefits sought—that is, what they actually *get* from consuming the product. Consumers in the 1960s—especially the late 1960s, as married women were moving back into the work force—put a much greater personal value on time saving than on healthy eating. The key point is that *the value that people see in any given bundle of attributes depends upon their own personal values.*

Who knew toothpaste could be so complicated? But understanding these tendencies is critical to competitive growth strategy development. Growth can be found in understanding these values more deeply, by both discovering new ways to connect with them and identifying where existing attributes no longer connect. To get to these insights, though, we need a process for exploring and uncovering customer value sought. That is where we head next.

Identifying and Analyzing Customer Value

A fundamental goal in the 3-Circle growth strategy process is to learn about customer value; first, estimating customer judgments from our own perspective, and then, obtaining customers' actual perceptions of value, importance, and beliefs about our firm and the competitive firm. There are a few key lessons in two separate areas that we will discuss here: executive estimates and actual customer self-reports.

Executive Estimates of Customer Value

For several reasons, it is initially very important for the executive team to provide their own estimates of customer value before getting feedback from customers.[11] First, it forces you and the team to think through the kinds of questions you will eventually ask of customers and how you might ask them. Second, in requiring the team to come to a consensus about expected customer evaluations, it may create conversations that have never really been explored before—vital conversations around the core value issues of the business. Finally, these estimates provide a foundation against which to compare actual customer beliefs that you obtain later. After you have conversations with customers, you may find that your team was right on the mark in anticipating customer perceptions. Alternatively, you may reveal areas in which your expectations were very different from what customers said. It is critical to note that in these differences exist potentially enormous growth opportunities. So, in this way, surprise is a good thing because it will help motivate the subsequent actions to close the gaps.

The first thing that must be done is to *estimate a list of customer reasons for choice*. You got some exposure to this in chapter 3 (recall the "service station A versus service station B" exercise). The way to do the exercise is to sit down for a 5- to 10-minute time frame and write down as many reasons you can think of why people would purchase your brand over the competitors. Then repeat the exercise, thinking of why customers might choose the competitive brand over yours. A key here is to pretend: *step into the shoes of your customers*.

Ultimately, reasons why people make choices will be stated as either attributes or benefits. To illustrate, consider that the president of a regional bank defined a project around the following context statement: "My goal is to figure out how *my bank* can grow by creating more value for and attracting *new small business loan and deposit clients* relative to their *current banks*."

Note that in a given region, there are many banking players, so market share is spread out over a variety of competitors. As such, this executive and his team felt it best to define the competitor as the "current bank" and to allow the target competitor to vary as needed. In the preliminary estimation of the reasons for choosing one bank over another for loan and deposit business, the bank's president surveyed nine different regional managers reporting to him, who, together, defined the following list:

- Timely service response
- High trust of bank and banker
- Knowledgeable employees
- Straight talk and sound advice
- Strong, stable, and secure bank
- Fair and open pricing
- Commitment to community service and involvement
- Decisions made locally
- Products and services offered
- Convenient locations

This is a very good list that covers both the numerator of the value ratio (i.e., benefits such as timeliness of service, trust, and security of the bank) and the denominator (i.e., fair and open pricing). As we will see, subsequent conversations with customers helped the team refine the list and statement of reasons. There are a couple of important pieces of advice here as you explore the reasons:

- *Break down reasons and attributes to concrete and actionable items.* In one major study, we found that parents would often state "quality of academics" in describing why they would choose a particular school over another. With some probing, we learned that the most significant subdimension of quality in this context was not the currency or sophistication of the curriculum or the textbooks used, or even the projects used. Instead, it was the *teacher's ability to communicate effectively* with the parents about the child's progress and the ability to respond to individual needs. Brainstorming ways to help teachers develop communication skills is straightforward. In contrast guessing how to improve "quality of academics" is not. So the advice here is to probe your initial list for actionable items. The acid test is to ask, "If the customers rated us poorly on this attribute, would we know what to do?"

- *Try to keep reasons and attributes simple.* Be careful not to use technical terms in describing reasons and attributes. The bank example demonstrates effective, customer-driven language. When executives take a first crack at this, however, they often use familiar jargon (e.g., technical features of an automobile like height of the suspension rather than consumer perceptions of ease of handling). Further, try to keep reasons simple and one-dimensional. For example, the bank president in our example would find it more precise to break the pricing dimension down into "fair pricing" and "open pricing." Because these are different dimensions, a customer could believe that pricing is fair but not open, for example. As such, estimating both together can be confusing.

Given a list of attributes and benefits, we would next have our executive team estimate customer perceptions of the *importance of those attributes*, as well as customer *beliefs about our brand and the competitive brand* on each dimension.[12]

- *Estimate importance of each attribute/benefit to customers.* "Importance" captures the evaluation, value, or weight people place on the dimensions of a given attribute or benefit.[13] To keep the task simple and fast, we have the executives we work with—and, later their customers—use a simple categorizing exercise in looking at importance. We ask them to rate attributes as low, medium, or high in importance. But the catch is they may not say that everything is important; we ask for discrimination. All attributes and benefits may seem to all be important—and, being the top 10, they most likely are—but it is still possible to discriminate the more from the less important in the list.
- *Estimate customer beliefs about our brand and competitive brand.* To understand how to think about beliefs, it is important to

understand the insights needed to effectively judge competitive positions. There are two relevant reference points:

○ *Ask how we do relative to the customers' expectations.* There is a long line of research in customer satisfaction that defines satisfaction as a customer judgment of how the firm performs compared to *what the customer expects.*[14] This notion of a relative judgment is very important. A lot of satisfaction research fails to take this into account. So if we find that customers rate us as 5.8 on a 7-point satisfaction scale, what do we know? Not much. It is much more informative to know whether customers believe we are below, above, or equal to their expectations.

○ *Ask how we do relative to the competitor.* In the late 1980s, management in AT&T's Allegheny region were consistent winners of the firm's internal satisfaction rewards, regularly scoring 98% in customer satisfaction. In contrast, the New York City region was consistently scoring in a percentage range around the mid-70s. Yet the Allegheny management team was eventually replaced while the New York team thrived, producing good business results. How could this be? Turns out the Allegheny region had tougher competition than did the New York region. In New York, AT&T was the dominant player. In Allegheny, competition was tougher. Allegheny produced high customer satisfaction scores because their current customers liked them, but customers liked competitors *even more* in many cases. In contrast, the New York team was able to produce positive sales and business results even though many of their customers were unhappy.[15] Two lessons are relevant here: (a) New York could be *even more* successful once they sorted out their satisfaction problems, but, more broadly, (b) Allegheny could only improve sales results by providing more value for customers than competitors did. *Competitor comparisons are at the core of customer judgment.*

Actual Consumer Interviews

The gathering of insights from customers is a critical step in developing growth strategy. It is not as difficult as it seems. Here are a few rules to guide the effort.

Rule 1: Just do it, even if it is only a small sample. For a start, interview 5 to 10 customers. Ironically, there is often initial resistance among executives to talk to customers about issues of value. The most common counterarguments are either "we already know what customers want" or "what will we be able to tell by talking to only a few customers?" The resistance is natural and logical. But this is one time when you need to suspend belief. In addition, it is not that difficult and costs very little. What do you ask? Essentially, you can ask the same basic questions that the members of the executive team just answered—(a) how important is each of the attributes and benefits on the list, and (b) how do customers evaluate our offer and the competitors' offers on those dimensions? When you are asking the right questions, you will find insight, even though such a sample is too small to make inferences about the larger population (see next paragraph). Open-ended interviews with customers—whether on the phone or in person—are thought provoking and may identify some obvious problems that require immediate exploration or even quick fixes. More generally, they will uncover issues that require deeper study and that even a small number of customers will really appreciate.

Rule 2: Don't get too carried away with your conclusions from small samples. So what happens once you actually sit down with a few customers? You obtain new insights that contrast, and may even contradict, your previous beliefs. In other words, you will learn. You also find that customers are appreciative. And you may see opportunities to make some short-term moves that will correct problems and improve your value. So we find a surprising aggressiveness among executives to act on this small-sample feedback because it tends to be powerful and energizing. Take care, though. It is not a good idea to make major investment decisions based on feedback from 1 or 5 or 10 customers. These initial interviews often, at best, provide you with a structure for further refining your hypotheses about the value customers seek from your organization. If well selected, insights from this small sample will (a) potentially have some immediate implications for fixing problems of which you were unaware, (b) identify longer-term growth opportunities to explore, and (c) provide the basis for further study with larger samples. We caution against running too far with the inputs from a small number of qualitative interviews without testing those conclusions on larger samples, however (unless those customers selected for the survey account for a significant portion of your company's revenue). The primary mandate is that those who you interview or survey are representative of the customer segment you have selected for the project.

Returning to our bank example, recall that the regional managers (RMs) for the bank estimated the following four attributes at the top of the list for small-business customers:

- Timely service response
- High trust of bank and banker
- Knowledgeable employees
- Straight talk and sound advice

In fact, the president conducted individual, in-depth exploratory interviews with a diverse group of seven small-business employees who had just started doing business with the bank during the previous 9 months (all from different industries). Interestingly, as a group, the small sample of business people framed the value they were looking for somewhat differently than the RMs. The small-business customers felt that the bank's unique value was tied to (a) the knowledge of its staff and their willingness to advise (as opposed to simply sharing knowledge), (b) the fact that the bank was locally owned and cared about its community, and (c) the *team approach* the bank used in providing service. There were two surprises. First, the importance of local community involvement was greater than the RMs expected. Second, the "team approach" did not even make the RMs' top-10 list of attributes but was of central importance to customers!

Now, why is the team approach important? Here is where we need to think deeply.[16] In the 3-Circle growth strategy process, *laddering* research is undertaken as a systematic effort to drill down into the needs and values that truly drive customer decision making. Laddering is a research method that might be described as "root-cause analysis" with customers. The method seeks to uncover the underlying values or reasons why certain attributes are important and influence decision making by asking, "why is that important?" in a sequence of questions. As an illustration, a team from the Infiniti automobile brand used laddering on 25 attributes of a new car design to "identify the core value embodied by or most closely associated with each feature."[17] Figure 4.3 shows the aggregate ladder that emerged when consumers were asked why they felt the "around view monitor" with video on all sides of the car was important. Based on the research across all the attributes, the strategy and planning teams were able to prioritize new features according to the core values of the target market and make feature rollout recommendations based on the laddering research. The Infiniti EX35 is the first model to have the around-view-monitor (AVM) feature.

In the banking case, laddering with the customer respondents revealed they were driven by both time and profitability (not surprising for small businesses!). Figure 4.4 provides the laddering results for the three top attributes, as identified by our bank president. Note that the bank's team approach creates value for small-business customers by leveraging the knowledge of many people (less likely to miss something), and also by creating a more efficient process. The truth is we could push this ladder further—with a couple more "whys"—we would likely find out that an efficient process is important because there are so many other things that a small-business person has on the plate, and that time is one of their most precious commodities.

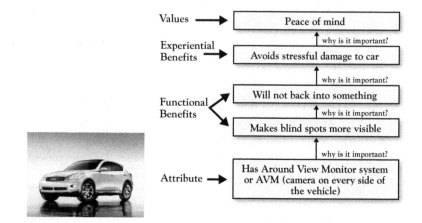

Figure 4.3. Ladder for Infiniti M35 design: Around view monitor.

Why the Client "Values" Our Bank

Figure 4.4. Ladders for small business bank customers.

It is important to note that the deeper values that you reach via laddering and other qualitative research techniques tend to reveal a lot about how we are hardwired as human beings. Across different countries and industries, the following types of values often emerge in laddering studies and other studies of values:

Accomplishment	Family
Belonging	Satisfaction
Self-fulfillment	Security, peace of mind
Self-esteem	Control

To illustrate, Figure 4.5 presents a ladder from a 3-Circle growth strategy study conducted by a research supplier that sells research services to brand managers in particular consumer-package-goods categories. Although a totally different context and a different attribute than the Infiniti (in this case, simply vendor familiarity), the end value is the same: peace of mind.

Chapter Summary

Among several implications that the bank took away from the 3-Circle analysis was the importance of building and reinforcing the team culture

Laddering Primary Attribute

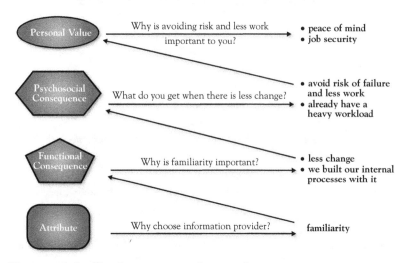

Figure 4.5. Ladder for customer of research services.

as their distinctive competitive advantage (what we call *Area A*). This involved creating new education programs and building in initiatives to proactively get clients and prospective clients in front of several different bank team members within relevant specialties.

One lesson from this chapter is that when you ask the right questions of customers, the insights that emerge are almost always actionable for growth. From the customer's perspective, value is essentially what one gets relative to what one gives, and growth opportunities emerge from developing a broader and deeper understanding of both numerator and denominator. Competitive markets evolve around a shifting definition of value, which places a great premium on the firm's ability to maintain a close eye on the value customers are seeking and how that is changing over time. There is nothing new in that message. But what is new (and needed) is a way to break down value and uncover the highest-priority growth ideas. We start with this issue in chapter 5.

CHAPTER 5

Sorting Value

Introduction: The Value of "Sorting"

Kraft Foods' Tang—the orange-flavored drink that Americans closely associate with astronauts and the space program—experienced 30% growth in 2009 in developing markets, including Asia, Latin America, and Eastern Europe.[1] It is instructive to note how the firm has leveraged different kinds of value in achieving these results. In competing in any market, there is some basic value a brand *must provide*, including adequate distribution and certain levels of market awareness and understanding of the product. Other dimensions of value *differentiate* the product; in Tang's case, it is a unique flavor and established brand equity. The company has new flavors, including mango variations in the Philippines and maracuja (passion fruit) in Brazil. As the brand reach was expanded, the company remained open to research and insight about unmet needs, and potentially *yet-to-be-determined* attributes. In China, they discovered both a strong belief that children's hydration was important and required drinking a lot of water (up to 6 glasses a day) and that kids found water boring! Most significantly, though, they found a strong preference for single servings, leading to the development of single-serve powder sticks to address this unmet need. This new form of packaging was adopted in place of pitcher packs, which Chinese moms found to provide *nonvalue* (in being wasteful and expensive).

At this point in the book, we have established the challenges of growing in the competitive marketplace today, introduced the 3-Circle model, and explored the basic concepts behind it. As reflected in the Tang example, we have also reinforced throughout that in any customer market, there are different *dimensions* of customer value that can play different strategic roles for the firm. Different strategy and customer value frameworks over the past 30 years have identified categories of value in disparate areas of the literature. Cutting across those frameworks[2] and adding unique insight around nonvalue, we can summarize these categories as follows:

- *Required but nondifferentiating attributes.* There are certain attributes that a firm *must have* to play the game. What is important about these basic attributes is that (a) their absence leads to customer dissatisfaction, because all competitors have them, and, for that reason, (b) they do not provide a basis for differentiation. In Theodore Levitt's words, a customer of strip steel not only expects a product that meets specifications but also expects the product has minimal requirements for delivery times, purchase terms, support, and ideas for improving efficiency. In contrast, the absence of these attributes leads to a significant drop in overall satisfaction.

- *Differentiating attributes.* Kano's model[3] suggests that there are two types of attributes that may provide a firm's basis for differentiation. The first are *performance* attributes, which are attributes that consumers expect but on which performance can vary. So while the Ford Escape Hybrid and the Jeep Compass are each characterized by fuel efficiency, the Escape gets a superior 31 miles per gallon. Performance attributes are those for which customers base their willingness to pay. But Kano's model also defines *excitement* attributes as those that may not be anticipated by customers. These are attributes whose absence does not lower customer satisfaction but whose presence may well significantly increase it.

- *Yet-to-be-determined attributes.* For hundreds of years, travelers carried suitcases. But there existed a latent demand for ease of transport. This was finally discovered and solved by a stewardess who jimmy-rigged wheels onto her suitcase. Other stewardesses followed suit, the luggage companies took note, and today it is difficult to find a suitcase that *does not* have wheels. Sometimes, potential new, desired attributes are known to both firm and customer. For example, for years, people walking around with a cell phone in one pocket and a PDA in another recognized the need for an integrated unit. But often, new ideas that better meet existing needs are a matter of discovery by firms (and customers!) who are continuously on the lookout.

There are three kinds of nonvalued attributes. Surprisingly, very important growth implications emerge from considering different attributes that are currently not valued by customers.

- *Nonvalue: Attributes that can be reduced or dropped with no loss in value.* In a case identified in Kim and Mauborgne's work, Accor developed a new hotel concept called "Formule 1" by taking out a number of dimensions of value they believed were not valued by a short-stay segment of the market. Accor eliminated fancy lobbies, restaurants and bars, workout rooms, and even the receptionist, who was replaced by an automated teller machine (ATM). They eliminated these values to invest heavily in the other attributes that were highly valued by this customer segment: quiet, clean rooms with excellent beds. Independently, the idea of eliminating nonvalue has emerged as a strategic theme in Jean-Claude Larreche's interesting work on the Momentum Effect model discussed in chapter 4.
- *Nonperformance: Attributes on which our performance fails to meet expectations.* In the Tang example, the pitcher packs required a parent to make a full pitcher, which led to waste. This is a good example of a feature that can be corrected (i.e., eliminated or changed) and an immediate positive boost to customer value may be provided.
- *Low awareness. Attributes that may have value to customers but are largely unknown.* It turns out that a very common reason why customers may see little value in a particular attribute or benefit is that they are simply not very aware of them.

In short, experience has shown that there is significant insight in recognizing these different categories of value in developing growth strategy. But what is needed is a way to simultaneously represent all of these categories of value in a manner that can be easily taught within the organization in order to get team members most quickly focused on the important dimensions of growth strategy.

We will describe a case study in order to illustrate how the 3-Circle framework provides the basis for integrating all of these value concepts in an actionable way.

The 3-Circle Model: Seven Categories of Value

The Amazon Kindle is the first-of-its-kind electronic reader that has now become the market standard. It allows for 1,500 book titles to be downloaded, voice or text reading, and utilizes a technology called "E Ink," which looks like print on paper and is clearly visible both indoors and outdoors. The Apple iPad, its biggest new threat, was introduced as a "truly magical and revolutionary product" by Apple CEO Steve Jobs in a highly anticipated media event on January 27, 2010. Jobs described the iPad as a third category of device, somewhere in the middle between a laptop and a smart phone. He described a product that was superior for web browsing, e-mail, photo management, video viewing, and video game playing. But he further described the iPad as "standing on the shoulders" of Amazon and its Kindle product, which he felt had done a great job of pioneering the e-book reading functionality. The iPad is linked directly to the iBooks store, has navigation that replicates page turning with an actual book, provides quick access to tables of contents, and has flexibility with font size and type (see Figure 5.1 for images of each device). Throughout the next section, we will use the iPad-versus-Kindle comparison as a basis for illustrating how value might be sorted in this category, using the comments of posters in a *Wall Street Journal* forum and other media sources.[4] The analysis here is framed as follows: What might be the basic elements of the growth strategy that Amazon might pursue with the Kindle in light of potential competition from Apples iPad? So our operational context statement here is, "Our goal is to determine how *Amazon* can defend and grow its Kindle sales by creating more value for *established e-book readers* than *Apple's iPad*."

Consider the ratings presented in Table 5.1, which was developed based on early popular press and blog comparisons of the Kindle and the iPad. We will use the comparison of these two products, as well as

Figure 5.1. iPad vs. Kindle: Comparing e-book readers.

Source: http://fictionwritersreview.com/essays/the-age-of-binary-bookmaking

other case examples, to illustrate how the dimensions of value in that developing market can be categorized.

Your job in the sorting exercise is to identify where these different dimensions of value belong in the 3-Circle framework. Figure 5.2 presents the generic "outside view" of the 3 circles, showing 7 categories of value. As we have noted, the upper right-hand circle represents customer needs and values; the upper left-hand circle represents *customer perception* of the value that our company provides; and the bottom circle represents customer perception of the competitor's value. Each of the 7 areas in the framework—indicated by the letters A through G—has strategic meaning. The task here is to sort the reasons or attributes that you have assessed into different areas.

Corresponding to the outside view of the 3-Circle model presented graphically in Figure 5.2, Table 5.2 provides some simple sorting rules. These rules identify how feedback from customers may be used to categorize particular attributes and benefits into the different areas of the model. The inputs for sorting are straightforward: a comparison of your firm's rating or evaluation (by customers) versus the competitor, qualified by attribute importance.

Table 5.1. Established E-Book User Ratings:* iPad vs. Kindle

Attribute/benefit	Perceived importance: L = low M = moderate H = high	iPad rating: How does this segment rate its expectations on the iPad on this attribute/benefit? 1 = below 2 = meets 3 = exceeds	Kindle rating: How does this segment rate its expectations on the Kindle on this attribute/benefit? 1 = below 2 = meets 3 = exceeds
Kindle Area A dimensions			
Reading fatigue, easy on the eyes	H	1	3
Battery life	H	2	3
Size, weight→ mobility	H	2	3
Operating costs (Internet access fees)	M	2	3
Purchase price	M	1	2
Area B dimensions			
Storage for books, material	H	2	2
Online access to reading material	H	2	2
iPad Area C dimensions			
Navigation	H	3	2
Use for magazines, colorful media	M	3	1
Use for video, movies	M	3	1
iPad Area F dimensions			
Breadth of applications	L	3	1

*Estimated based on trade accounts and user commentary, March 2010

Judgment of value is broken down by attribute or reason. Each individual attribute is sorted into Areas A through F based on the relative ratings given by customers (first column) qualified by our assessment of attribute importance. Area G is somewhat a unique area that explores attributes or attribute levels that might not currently exist in the market. We will later elaborate further on Area G. Figure 5.3 provides a graphical representation of the data in Table 5.1.

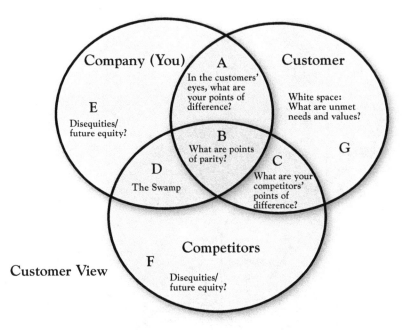

Figure 5.2. Three circles: The outside view.

Table 5.2. Sorting Rules: Identifying Categories of Value

Customer's assessment of us vs. competitor	Attribute importance	Area into which attribute/reason would be sorted
Better than competitor	High	Area A
Same as competitor	Moderate-high	Area B
Worse than competitor	High	Area C
Both below expectations	Low	Area D
We are below expectations; competitor is better	Any level	Area E
Competitor is below expectations; we are better	Any level	Area F
Both are below expectations Brainstorm; what problems have you heard about, what unmet needs exist, what value might be added?	Moderate-high	Area G

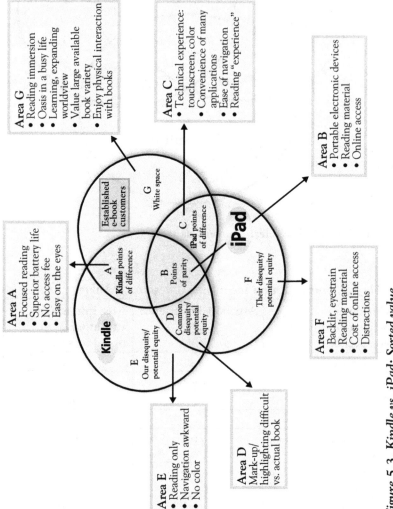

Area G
- Reading immersion
- Oasis in a busy life
- Learning, expanding worldview
- Value large available book variety
- Enjoy physical interaction with books

Area C
- Technical experience: touchscreen, color
- Convenience of many applications
- Ease of navigation
- Reading "experience"

Area B
- Portable electronic devices
- Reading material
- Online access

Area A
- Focused reading
- Superior battery life
- No access fee
- Easy on the eyes

Area F
- Backlit, eyestrain
- Reading material
- Cost of online access
- Distractions

Area E
- Reading only
- Navigation awkward
- No color

Area D
- Mark-up/ highlighting difficult vs. actual book

Figure 5.3. Kindle vs. iPad: Sorted value.

Areas B, A, C

The iPad is an improved netbook, but it won't replace our Kindle.

—Jon Kamp, February 12, 2010

The first three areas of the model under consideration address attributes the firm has in common with their competitor and those on which there are competitive differences.

Area B: Points of parity. We begin with Area B because most contemporary discussions of customer value begin with the point that there are elements of value that are *must haves,* without which a firm cannot even compete. Area B captures the *required, nondifferentiating attributes* that are common to the competitors in the market. They are currently nondifferentiating.

Identifying Area B: Points of parity. In customer research, points of parity are at least moderately important attributes and benefits on which customers rate you and your competitor as basically the same.[5] There is a sense of equivalence. In the most current *Consumer Reports* study of consumer perception of automotive brands, for example, Ford and Subaru were in a virtual dead heat for second place, with 22% and 21% of consumers rating them in the top three on safety, the most important attribute to consumers.[6] So in an evaluation of Ford versus Subaru, safety is a wash; that is, the two are not distinguishable on this dimension. The Kindle and the iPad have a number of basic characteristics in common— by way of description, they are both portable electronic devices that can be used for reading books and other material. One nondifferentiating element for which the two might be similarly rated would be online access to reading material—each provides access to various book titles and other media remotely—the iPad through wireless Internet access and the Kindle through a 3G network.

Areas A and C: Points of difference. This is the central definition of competitive advantage as perceived by customers. Very simply, Area A captures the value that we provide customers that (a) matters to them, and (b) is different than the value competitors provide. Area C, then, is essentially the competitive complement to Area A. On what important advantages does the competitor hang its hat?

Identifying Areas A and C. It is usually fairly easy to identify the attributes and benefits that go into Areas A and C. These attributes tend to stand out in customers' minds. Area A attributes and benefits are those of high importance for which our firm rates as superior to the competition. Area C is the flip side—important attributes and benefits on which the competitor is rated as superior. Returning to the 2010 automobile data from *Consumer Reports*, it is no surprise that safety is the predominant Area A item for Volvo (73%) against every other brand in the market. In a direct comparison with Toyota, though, the *Consumer Reports* data suggest that Volvo's Area A dominance of safety might be trumped by Toyota's superior scores on leadership in quality, value, and environmental friendliness, all among the top five important attributes.

Users of e-book very clearly identify the trade-offs between the Kindle and the new iPad; these would be the key Area A and Area C attributes representing the "get" and "give" of each device. While the less sophisticated of the two devices, with far less functionality, the Kindle has a simplicity that is perceived to be a core strength—it focuses on reading, *undistracted by e-mail, the web, and gaming opportunities*:

> When I want to disconnect and read, I can't have distractions, and having a multifunction device has always been an avenue for distractions to me.[7]

> When I want to read, I want undistracted reading. As it is I don't have much time to do so, with an iPad, it just defeats the purpose.[8]

There are two other major points of difference for the Kindle, reflected in the Table 5.1 ratings: much superior battery life (1 week vs. iPad's 10 hours) and no monthly fee for Internet access, significantly reducing operating costs. Most significant, though, among e-book users may be the fact that the Kindle is easier on the eyes because of its E-Ink technology. In contrast, the iPad's backlit screen presentation is believed to create eyestrain:

> The iPad, unlike the rest of the e-book readers has a traditional backlit screen and it is more tiring to the eyes. I cannot imagine people taking it to the coffee shops to read for a long time.[9]

In all, we might summarize the Kindle's points of difference around the phrase "focused reading experience." The commentary of loyal Kindle users reflects a deep commitment to reading as an important lifestyle activity, and a devotion to the Kindle as a means of delivering content.

In contrast, there is some attention given to the iPad for its unique features (Area C). In the reading domain, two major points of difference for the iPad are its navigation and page-turning capabilities, as well as its full color feature, which enhances reading of color-rich media:

> I've been waiting for a convenient way to read my collection of PDFs and Zinio magazines, as well as eBooks, and the iPad is just the ticket. As a long time user of eBooks (I had an original Rocket eBook, and have its successor, the eBookWise), the iPad definitely has my attention.[10]

The ratings in Table 5.1 reflect these advantages, along with a couple of the more obvious iPad advantages, which predominantly focus on the wide range of applications for its iPhone (videos, games, photography). In fact, consumers who value this dimension look at the iPad as a "Kindle Killer":

> The iPad is a Kindle killer. No question about it. For about $200 more you get a device that goes way, way beyond the capabilities of a Kindle. Coupled with the Apple/iPod/iPhone/iTouch name recognition and the iPad is going to sell like crazy. Every kid in college is going to want an iPad.[11]

We can see that there is a segment of dedicated e-book readers who will cede the greater capability and applications benefit to iPad, but who will not find those features to be important. The Table 5.1 analysis provides a fair accounting of the relative competitive position of each device, and the analysis is relatively straightforward. Areas D, E, F, and G take a bit more interpretation.

Areas D, E, F: Disequity or Potential Equity?

Areas D, E, and F represent the interesting and important space that is *outside the customer's circle*, as we have defined it. In fact, it is usually not immediately obvious what factors that we categorize into these areas actually mean, because there are multiple meanings. An attribute or benefit is placed outside the customer's circle may represent one of four cases:

- The current offering is unsatisfactory to the customer on this attribute (disequity).
- The attribute is unimportant to the customer (nonvalued equity).
- The customer does not really understand the attribute or benefit and how effectively we offer it (miscommunicated equity).
- We do not effectively provide the value sought, but we possibly could (unleveraged equity). This is an important phenomenon that is addressed in detail in chapter 7, so is given less attention here.

Understanding these four distinctions is critical. This represents one layer of the analysis. But another critical part of the categorization is distinguishing whether this value that falls outside of the customer's circle is a concern for (a) just our firm, which puts it in Area E; (b) just the competitor, which puts it in Area F; or (c) *both* firms, which puts it in Area D, also known as "the swamp."[12] Let us consider these categories in more detail:

- *Nonvalued equity.* There are often attributes or benefits that are of great significance to a firm that fails to stir customers, and some that may even produce a negative reaction. For example, a well-known golf course architect was enamored with the idea of building an authentic Scottish golf experience at a particular American university. The course was designed to be relatively long, had no par set up on the scorecard, and was designed to be a course that patrons walked. The course was beautifully laid out within the land that the architect had to work with, complete with long grass, rolling fairways, and large, chunky pins on the large greens. The downside was the discovery (luckily, early enough in the process) of big concerns from potential patrons, for example, alumni coming to play on football weekends. These golfers, to put it mildly, were not inclined to spend 5 or 6 hours walking a long golf course prior to tailgating on football Saturday. So, as a last minute addition, designers had to squeeze in cart paths on the course and revamp a pro shop building with storage for electric carts underneath. Nonvalued equity is often discovered in personal discussions with customers that reveal relatively low interest or emphasis on certain dimensions of value the firm thought important.

- *Unsatisfactory delivery.* If your brand "underdelivers" relative to customer expectations, it has disequity. This is straightforward. So the car that promises 24 miles per gallon and delivers 18 disappoints in a manner similar to the restaurant that promises a 15-minute wait time that turns into 30 minutes. These sorts of issues may be easy to spot; you just have to ask. Disequity due to underperformance can be common to all competitors—like long waiting times in doctor's offices—and this may potentially be an Area G item (i.e., an unmet need). Alternatively, such disequity may be unique to one or another competitor. One example would be the viruses and system crashes experienced by Microsoft Windows, humorously pointed out by Apple in its clever Mac vs. PC ad campaign. Often, one competitor's advantages (e.g., Kindle's Area A—the electronic ink and ease of reading) are a reflection or mirror image of a competitor's disadvantage (e.g., iPad's Area F—the backlit screen and eye strain).

- *Customer is not aware of or does not understand the equity.* One of the most common things we find from the customer analysis in the 3-Circle process is that the firm has overestimated what its customers actually know about it. For example, recall that Pastor Buss and his team at Glenview New Church School (chapter 2) were surprised by a general lack of awareness of the school's vision and value proposition among prospective parents and even church members. Regarding iPad, we might speculate that given all the device can do, the photo management capability may get less attention than it deserves, given firmly established habits around photo management on laptops and PCs.

- *Unleveraged equity—the firm has a hidden capability to correct the current dissatisfying performance or serve an unmet need.* A particular attribute or benefit may in fact be a disequity because it is not currently delivered well. However, the firm *may* have the capability to deliver that value more effectively. This can be a major insight, and great efficiency when the firm discovers that its capability in one area may be able to compensate in another product market.

Note that each of these four states could be firm-specific (Area E or F) or could be a problem, concern, or opportunity faced by all competitors (Area D) that simply has not been resolved.

Identifying Area D, E, F Attributes and Benefits

The core definition of the value in Areas D, E, and F is that it is (a) deficient, (b) unimportant, or (c) not well known to the customer. Your ability to identify value that goes into these areas is dependent upon the method used. One approach that we have applied in the ratings in Table 5.1 is to ask customers to evaluate each competitive option on each attribute or benefit as either meeting, exceeding, or falling below expectations. So *deficiency or disequity* would be captured by *below-expectations* ratings. Any ratings on attributes or benefits that are deemed of moderate or high importance should be explored in more detail. The best example in the Kindle-iPad case is the fact that, with a certain segment of diehard e-book readers, the iPad's substantial capabilities in accessing other applications much like the iPad actually creates *disequity*, as noted earlier, by providing potential distractions from the reading experience.

An even more direct illustration of disutility or deficiency comes from Barnes & Noble's initial e-book entry called Nook, introduced in the fall of 2009. The Nook's positive points of difference are interesting—it replicates the Kindle's E-Ink technology, but with a *color touch screen*, providing more intuitive navigation for those accustomed to touch-screen technology. The package deal for the Nook also includes a book-sharing feature, allowing users to borrow books from one another rather than buying the books separately. However, a *BusinessWeek* review captures a critical disequity for the Nook: "Amazon's current-model Kindle 2 takes about three seconds from the moment you release the power button until you can start reading. On the Nook, it takes a minute and 50 seconds."[13] Page turning and navigation in the new Nook appear to be similarly sluggish.

Low attribute importance is also a reason why certain value dimensions may fall outside the customer's circle. This is, of course, captured in the importance ratings using our simple method of asking for a low, medium, or high rating. It should be noted that there are more sophisticated ways to obtain importance ratings, as it may be difficult for customers to be completely objective in these ratings. The challenge with self-report measures, which capture customer estimates of importance directly, is that customers may often rate all attributes of high importance. The analyst will need to use some judgment here based on the traditional meaning of importance as well as the stage of the life cycle in which this attribute might be categorized (see chapter 8 on dynamics). For example, once many battery manufacturers had adopted a self-testing capability for household batteries, it became clear, over time, that this was not a product benefit that consumers valued. Crystal Pepsi (a clear cola) is another example of an attempt to create a differentiating attribute that failed because it held no value for consumers.

Finally, certain attributes or benefits *may not be known* to customers. These attributes reveal themselves in discussions with customers. When you excitedly ask customers to rate your brand on its postpurchase follow-up service (which you know to be excellent) and they say "what service?" you know you have hit on an Area E attribute.

Area G: The White Space

The "white space" captures unmet customer needs. While the internal language of most businesses tends to be around existing attributes—for example, the offer you currently produce—potentially profitable value often comes from thinking from the view of customer problems, needs, and values, which are not currently addressed. These are the deeper reasons why customers purchase those attributes. Area G represents value that does not currently exist in the market but that is (or would be) desired by customers. It suggests that there is some degree of elasticity in the customer's definition of value, portions of which neither the firm nor its competitors have yet discovered.

There are two kinds of value in Area G. There are attributes or benefits that the *customer can articulate but that do not currently exist*. For example, new product ideas such as wheels on suitcases, televisions with built-in DVD players, and cell phones with web access and calendar tools were obtained from innovative customers. Alternatively, Area G may contain value that has not yet been discovered, that is, *new attributes unanticipated by consumers* whose value production can only been seen with experience. Herein lies an opportunity for growth.

The identification of Area G puts into our shared language an ongoing space that can be continuously explored and mined for new value-creation opportunities. The ideas that may appear in Area G can be identified a variety of ways:

- *Direct questioning.* It is possible to directly ask a customer what our unmet needs are. What can we do better? What can we do that would make you a more satisfied customer? A couple of challenges with direct questions like these are that (a) usually, when asked, customers are not in the state of mind in which they have experienced concerns or unmet needs before and so cannot access relevant thoughts, or (b) they ask for the world.

- *Customer complaints.* Many times, customer complaints for a firm reflect Area E items, such as, current disequities or deficiencies. However, it is possible that a consumer complaint may be the tip of the iceberg, and discovering the iceberg represents a real opportunity for growth. For example, a 2004 study by the Better Business Bureau identified the three most common complaints in the mobile phone industry to involve (a) billing, (b) the quality of customer service, and (c) misrepresentation or miscommunication by sales or customer service personnel. Interestingly, complaints were often generated about the complaint-handling process itself, where "it was not uncommon for small misunderstandings . . . to balloon into much larger customer service issues, enraging the customers

and, in many cases, overwhelming the original issue."[14] There
are clearly root causes underlying customer dissatisfaction that
can be addressed.

- *Qualitative research.* While studying customer complaints and
  having direct conversations with customers will provide insight
  into unmet needs, customers cannot always put their finger on
  what ails them. Instead, inferences must often be made from
  more general conversations about understanding larger problems and concerns that the customer has, research approaches
  that dig beneath the surface to understand customer needs
  and values, and ethnographic studies that observe customers
  and the circumstances surrounding their consumption of the
  product.[15] Detailing these methods is beyond the scope of the
  current book. However, the laddering research discussed in
  chapter 4 is one illustration of this type of research.

- *Observing customer-to-customer conversations.* There is significant insight into deeper customer needs in online customer
  communities. Such communities provide opportunities for
  customers to engage each other through discussion boards, surveys, photo galleries, and other online events around a particular common interest. Communispace is one organization that
  provides online community development and management
  capability. Working with Charles Schwab,[16] for example, Communispace built an online customer community that revealed
  several important insights into the unmet investment needs of
  gen Xers (those born between 1961 and 1981). These unmet
  needs included their need for financial guidance, their distrust
  of investment service firms, their disdain for firms seeking
  to discuss retirement, and their need for advice on managing expenses and saving rather than strictly investing. Schwab
  responded with some creative new accounts and services
  targeted at this market, generating new sales as well as loyalty
  to those who appreciated the fact that the company listened.

What are some Area G items for e-book readers? One way to explore
this is to ladder on the Area A dimensions. That is, ask this customer segment why, for example, *focused reading* is such an important dimension

to them. One can envision that dedicated e-book readers would reflect that focused reading allows them to make every minute reading more productive and enjoyable. Why is that important? For some, it may be that reading is a comfortable oasis in a busy life, so the goal is to separate one's self from the current busy world in which they live for respite. In addition, there is likely to be deep personal interest and connections with the authors and topics about which they read. There is, to some degree, deep immersion in the work. Such immersion may be associated with the desire for understanding geographic locations in the book, more about the author and his or her background and other works, or deeper insight into particular historical events in the work. What services or ideas might enhance such a *reading immersion* experience? How about links to social networks or blogs dedicated to particular authors or genres? How about information about the history of countries and locations in which books are set? How about information about events related to the book and author? There are likely many ideas, but the point is that identifying profitable growth opportunities significantly benefits from a deep understanding of the goals and values that drive interest in this consumption experience. It may be that the firm who really understands the depth of the reader's values will be the one to develop the most grounded new ideas that are most likely to connect with customers.

Overall Positioning Strategy

By the time you have been able to explore the value that customers seek in some depth, you will be able to come to some conclusions about your offering's *overall position* as perceived by customers and potential customers. The position of a product or service is essentially a summary assessment of where it resides in the mind of customers. Much like a city resides in the space defined in a map with distances relative to other cities, your offering exists somewhere in customers' minds in a space relative to other competitive offerings. One tool that has become increasingly common for representing competitive positions is what is called a "value map." The first representation of a value map appeared in the work of Rangan and Kasturi in 1992.[17] Figure 5.4 provides an example of a value map with selected e-book-reader brands. The two dimensions of the map match the dimensions of the simple "value = benefits/cost" equation. The horizontal dimension captures some the *benefits* provided by each offering. The vertical axis captures *selling price*, which, in many product and service categories, accounts for a large proportion of the customer's cost. These dimensions might be estimated based on completely objective criteria.[18] Alternatively, they could be measured based on customer *perception* of price and benefits. In either case, the benefits dimension is generally an aggregation of customer perception or objective measures across many different features or dimensions. The value map in Figure 5.4 is estimated based on the objective ratings and prices provided in *Consumer Reports'* latest assessment of e-book readers. The map generally reflects a positive relationship between benefits provided and price, with the Nook and the Kindle anchoring the lower left quadrant and the iPad distanced from the other brands in the upper right. The Kindle 2 (costing $260, on average) is a substantially better value than Barnes & Noble's Nook at the same price (recall the challenges with Nook's speed of response). The iPad far exceeds the other options on a variety of dimensions, driven by its advantages on versatility and file support. Hence, the value map illustrates the likely trade-offs between additional benefits that customers receive and the prices they may be willing to pay. Mapping a market over time is often eye-opening, as one can track the competitive changes in pricing and product features and make some judgments about what customers value, particularly if the map is based on customer perception. We introduce the value map tool here so we can use it again in chapter 6. There, we will use the value map to characterize the positioning implications of particular growth strategies that emerge out of the 3-Circle analysis.

Chapter Summary: Not All Value Is Created Equal

This chapter has been about categories of value. The reason that we seek to understand and "sort" value is that not all value is the same. And, as we will soon see, there are different growth strategies for different categories of value. To give a little prelude to this, consider that the key focus of both Porter's framework on competitive advantage and the resource-based view of the firm can be framed as *Area A* strategies:

- Grow, strengthen, and defend Area A, our unique points-of-difference.

Price

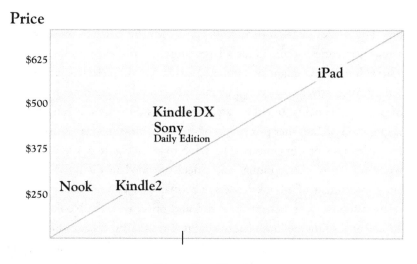

Benefits/Performance

Figure 5.4. Value map: Selected E-book readers.*

*Data on which this value map is based come from *Consumer Reports'* ratings of e-book readers on the dimensions of readability, versatility, responsiveness, page turn, navigation, file support, and size of viewer display, weighted equally. The figures used for the iPad are estimated based on initial reports, as the iPad was not included in the full ratings of the e-book readers.

Sources: http://www.consumerreports.org/cro/electronics-computers/phones-mobile-devices/e-book -readers/e-book-reader-ratings/ratings-overview.htm; http://www.consumerreports.org/cro/magazine -archive/2010/june/electronics-computers/computers/apple-ipad/index.htm

- However, by sorting value into the categories defined in the 3-Circle model, there are several other equally important strategies that might be pursued. These strategies include the following:
  - o Maintain and defend critical points of parity (Area B).
  - o Correct, reduce, and eliminate disequities, or reveal equities that customers are unaware of (Areas E and D).
  - o Potentially neutralize competitors' differentiation (Area C).
  - o Identify totally new value identified around customers' unmet needs (Area G).

And importantly, these five categories of growth strategy can often be pursued *in parallel*, as a portfolio of strategies to accelerate growth by providing a big jump in customer value. We dig into these growth strategies in the next chapter.

CHAPTER 6

Growth Strategy

Introduction

We have used the phrase "breakdown" value several times so far. The term *breaking down* has become a common phrase in the English language in reference to dividing some whole up into component parts. In sports, one of the most impressive feats in the history of breaking down complexity is Ben Hogan's classic *Five Lessons: The Modern Fundamentals of Golf*.[1] Mr. Hogan is one of the greatest champions in the history of the game, with 64 PGA tour wins between 1938 and 1959. These included nine major tournament titles, six of which came after a horrific 1949 accident in which the car he was driving collided head on with a Greyhound bus. In *Five Lessons*, he provides the first in-depth accounting of the golf swing broken down into four core elements: the grip, stance and posture, first part of the swing (backswing), and the second part of the swing (downswing). This paperback has itself turned into a modern classic, still in print (available on Amazon!) and responsible for the swings of some of the most accomplished players today, including Tiger Woods.

Those inexperienced with golf often wonder how this seemingly simple game can be worthy of such devotion and study. They are incredulous to learn, for example, that Mr. Hogan's book has an entire chapter on *the grip*—that is, simply how to hold the club! Figure 6.1 shows the striking ink drawings by Anthony Ravielli on the cover of *Sports Illustrated*, perfect in detail as Mr. Hogan demanded. Hogan's devotion to studying different approaches to gripping the club has him describing grip aesthetics in words rich with emotion: "For myself and other serious golfers there is an undeniable beauty in the way a fine player sets his hands on the club." Such admiration and attention to subtle nuance is the result of deep

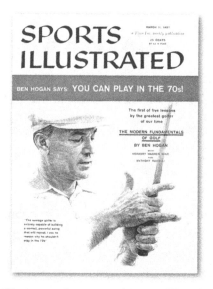

Figure 6.1. Ben Hogan on the cover of Sports Illustrated.

study, and it leads to explanations of the grip of such a technical nature as to leave any but the most dedicated student of golf scratching heads:

> When a golfer has completed his left-hand grip, the V formed by the thumb and forefinger should point to his right eye. The total pressure of all the fingers should not be any stronger (and may even be a little less strong) than the pressure exerted by just the forefinger and the palm pad in the preparatory guiding action. In the completed I grip, the main pressure points are the last three fingers, with the forefinger and the palm pad adding assisting pressure. (Hogan, 1957)

Yet Mr. Hogan is also clear in identifying the important *outcomes* of developing this understanding, which ultimately connects the grip with other parts of the swing:

> Keeping pressure on the shaft with the palm pad does three things: it strengthens the left arm throughout the swing; at the top of the backswing, the pressure from this pad prevents the club from

slipping from the player's grasp; and it acts as a firm reinforcement at impact. (Hogan, 1957)

The grip elements represent one piece of the puzzle. But Mr. Hogan has a deep, almost stunning insight about the outcome of grounding your golf swing in solid fundamentals throughout. Ultimately, careful attention to the grip helps in executing other fundamental elements of the swing and also dramatically improves the golfer's ability to *compete*:

> Frequently, you know, what looks like a fairly good golf swing falls apart in competition . . . the harsh light of competition reveals that a swing is only superficially correct . . . It can't stand up day after day. A correct swing will. In fact, the greater the pressure you put on it, the better your swing should function, if it is honestly sound. (Hogan, 1957)

While we would overly flatter ourselves to suggest that we could replicate the level of depth and expertise in Mr. Hogan's work on the golf swing in the study of growth strategy, our intent is the same. The 3-Circle model is about creating honestly sound strategy that will hold up under competition. We do that by breaking down value, seeking to deeply understand the component parts and how to work with them and then assembling them back together in an integrative strategy. The primary insight is that each individual category of value can spawn unique ideas for growth through building the firm's ability to produce and communicate value that really matters to customers. This is what we will be breaking down in this chapter.

Value and Positioning

There are a number of prescriptions for growth that emerge from the 3-Circle model. However, growth strategy should not be developed independent of the firm's overall positioning strategy. At the end of chapter 5, the value map was presented as a means of thinking through where your offering lies in a value space, defined by price on one axis and perceived benefits on the other. Growth strategy ideas that each seek to improve value for customers should form an integrative whole to the extent possible, and should be consistent with the overall positioning and meaning for your organization or brand. As you think through growth strategies, it is important to do so with the backdrop of your goals for your overall position as a choice alternative for the customer. The overall goal of the analysis is to improve the value proposition for the customer relative to competitors to increase the probability that the customer will choose your offering.

Overall Positioning Strategy

We have replicated the value map from chapter 5 into Figure 6.2, which illustrates "directional" moves from a center location. As noted in chapter 5, a firm improves its value proposition by either *adding or improving benefits* or *lowering the customer's costs*. The degree to which adding or improving benefits (moving *east* on the value map) increases sales depends on whether those benefits are important to customers. The degree to which changing customer costs or price will affect sales depends on customer price sensitivity. Lowering customer costs represents a *southerly* move, while raising customer costs is a move toward the *north* on the map. However, simultaneous changes in both numerator and denominator can occur—then, customer response depends on the combined impact on value. So a firm might add benefits and raise price, which would move it *northeast* on the 45-degree line on the map, as when Ford makes a hybrid version of its Escape SUV and charges $9,000 more. Alternatively, a *southwest* move would involve reducing benefits compared to an existing position and lowering price, illustrated by a cluster of emergent cell phone and cell phone service providers like Net10 who sell simple cell phones on prepaid plans at prices substantially lower than the standard national carriers. Figure 6.3 illustrates a unique strategy by Apple, moving the iPhone southeast—enhancing both benefits (twice as fast) and cost (half the price). We will see that this overall value positioning is difficult but increasingly evident, reflected in Kim and Mauborgne's work on value innovation and blue ocean strategy.[2] In sum, while we think of individual changes as additions or deletions of attributes or benefits, such changes, in fact, (a) may have multiple elements, and (b) will eventually be translated in the minds of customers to some sense of overall value for the money. The degree to which such changes contribute to improved profitability is a function of both changes in sales revenue and changes in cost.

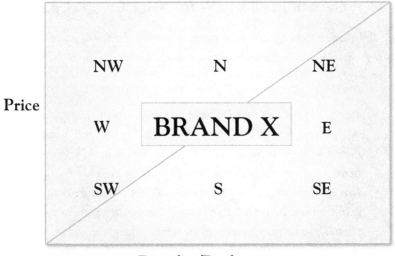

Figure 6.2. Directional moves on the value map.

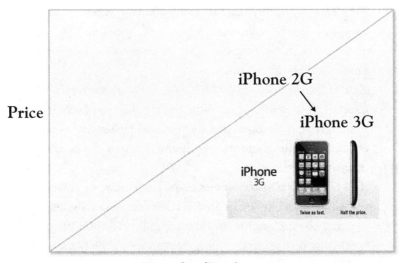

Figure 6.3. Repositioning the iPhone 3GS: "Twice as fast. Half the Price."

Growth Implications for Value Categories

In alphabetical order, here is a generally comprehensive list of the key growth strategy implications from the seven value categories in the 3-Circle framework:

- *Area A: Defend and build.* The chief goal is to enhance and enlarge Area A relative to Area C by building distinctive attributes and benefits for which we have a unique capability or identity, in a manner focused on target customers.
- *Area B: Maintain and defend the foundation.* There are core attributes and benefits (table stakes) that you must deliver *as effectively* as competitors do to even be in the game.
- *Area C: Shore up your value (i.e., neutralize competitors' advantage) where it is cost-effective and strategy-consistent to do so.* Certain deficits in Area C may provide an opportunity to improve our value proposition by neutralizing and perhaps exceeding the competitor's advantage. Alternatively, live and let live.
- *Areas D, E: Correct negative value, eliminate or reduce unwanted attributes, better communicate, or find new capabilities.* These are areas with multiple dimensions for which there are a variety of growth strategy directions.
- *Area F: Improve upon and exploit the competitor's unique deficiency.* This is a strategic decision, but it holds the possibility of improving your offering's value position by helping customers discover more about what is legitimately wrong with the competitor's offering.
- *Area G: Continually seek unmet needs.* There are ways in which the white space can be explored in a structured and disciplined manner. The exploration provides a means of uncovering potentially new sources of value that can substantially improve customers' connection with the firm's offering.

Here, we will cycle through these ideas, expanding upon them and introducing a number of illustrations. An important point here is that there is a logical sequence or order with which one should evaluate growth opportunities. We are going to suggest a series of strategic growth options—questions that will prompt a concrete look at a number of potential ideas for growing the value customers receive that will enhance and strengthen the firm's overall position. We always need to keep in mind the simple value formula and the goal: to enhance that overall value by recognizing that the firm might improve either numerator or denominator:

$$\text{value}_j = \frac{\text{benefits}_j}{\text{cost}_j} .$$

We will walk through each of the imperatives and strategic growth opportunities, one at a time. We will occasionally refer to "numerator" ideas, which are ideas to build and enhance benefits. "Denominator" ideas are those related to reducing customer costs—either direct costs or effort costs.

Overall Positioning: First, Take a Hard, Honest Look at Your Area A

The following questions are among the most essential that one can ask about the business that can be answered by the customer value analysis you have completed:

- What is our unique equity with customers? Do we truly have a unique competitive advantage?
- If no, why not?
- If yes, does that Area A value accurately capture the market position we are trying to reflect?
- Going forward, what do we want Area A to be—that is, what points of difference do we want to establish?

To illustrate a common finding, consider a manufacturer who has, for the past several years, touted its *efficiency* as its primary point of difference. The firm's management has been consistent in communicating this priority both internally (mission statement, coffee cups, posters on the wall) and externally with distributors and customers, proud of the fact that it is the "most efficient in the industry." Then, in a 3-Circle growth project, some leaders in the firm discover the surprising insight that customers only care about the firm's efficiency if they see some benefit from it. In some ways, the firm's promotion of its efficiency is almost resented by some customers who do not believe they see anything being passed down in the way of lower costs or greater efficiency for them. Recall similar cases in this book (e.g., Resource Recovery Corporation, Food Supplier, Inc.) in which executives discovered that their Area A was not nearly as large and distinctive as they had envisioned. So the first step in plotting growth is to get a clear understanding of your current Area A, being open to the possibility that customers may not view you as you think they do. As noted in chapter 5, an important element of this assessment is identifying where you currently reside in consumers' minds on the value map. Table 6.1 summarizes this first priority.

Exploring Five Growth Imperatives

The strategic positioning assessment is critical in highlighting strategic priorities for the company. In addition, there are some tactical insights that emerge that can be fixed in a straightforward way. The fundamental growth imperatives can be summarized as follows:

- Correct obvious, critical deficiencies (Areas E, D)
- Solidify Area B
- Neutralize Area C

Table 6.1. First Priority in Growth Strategy: Assess Your Area A

Growth strategy imperative	Question summary	Case examples
• Take a hard, honest look at your Area A	• What is our unique equity with customers? Do we truly have a unique competitive advantage? • If no, why not? What do we want Area A to be? • If yes, does that Area A value accurately capture or reflect the market position we are trying to reflect? • Going forward, what do we want Area A to be (i.e., what points of difference do we want to establish)?	• "Efficiency" positioning • Resource Recovery Corporation • Food Supplier, Inc.

- Reduce and eliminate, or reinvigorate, current Areas E and D dimensions
- Build and defend Area A

The goal of 3-Circle analysis is to leverage the insight from the initial, structured analysis of customer feedback into a preliminary set of ideas or brainstorms about growth. We will provide a systematic walk-through of these ideas. Table 6.2 summarizes the analysis of the first four growth imperatives.

Table 6.2. Growth Imperatives 1 Through 4

Growth strategy imperative	Question summary	Case examples
1. Correct obvious deficiencies (Area E → Area B)	• What are current deficiencies we have that can impact customer value significantly (and may have a low cost of fixing)?	• Chocolate manufacturer • Domino's • Microsoft Windows 7 • Rolling Stone
2. Solidify/update Area B	• Are any Area B attributes maturing, changing?	• Computer memory
3. Neutralize Area C (Area C → Area B or Area C → Area A)	• What are the costs and benefits of matching a competitor's position in an area in which we currently do not compete or perhaps are deficient? • What current competitor advantages might actually be converted to an advantage for our firm?	• Burger King (Sausage McMuffin with Egg) • Airlines matching SWA's hedging • Droid catching up to and surpassing iPhone • Acquisitions • Hire away people (e.g., Lebron James; LA Kings got Wayne Gretzky; Brett Favre to Vikings; Phil Jackson) • Continental's purchase of Motorola's automotive electronics division (including OnStar) • Delta bought Northwest, United buys US Airways—leapfrogging that technology
4. Reduce and eliminate nonvalued benefits (Areas E and D)	• Are there any customer attributes/benefits that we might reduce or even eliminate that would have little impact on customer value? (cf. Kim and Mauborgne 1997)	• Formule 1 • Quicken

Growth Imperative 1: Correct Deficiencies (Areas E and D)

As we emphasize throughout the book, customer value is enhanced (by way of the numerator of the value ratio) by ensuring that the product substantively delivers upon and exceeds expectations. At times, there are very fundamental issues that emerge in research and analysis that suggest obvious change—for example, the proverbial low-hanging fruit. Note such insights occur both for substantive changes in quality and basic issues on which our current superiority is not being effectively communicated. A few examples include substantively changing benefits and clarifying customer perception.

Substantively Changing Benefits

In Michael Porter's work on competitive strategy and the value chain, he notes an example of a bulk chocolate manufacturer who sells its finished product to a confectionary producer in bulk bars.[3] Essentially, a study of the customer's inbound logistics and operations (i.e., the real processes and needs) led to the discovery that the chocolate manufacturer was wasting time hardening and packaging the chocolate, when the confectionary producer had to remelt it upon arrival. Each manufacturer saved time and money when the chocolate manufacturer began delivering the product in liquid form. This illustrates a reality in most firm-customer relationships—there very often exist opportunities to improve value (sometimes for both parties) that are surprisingly related to basic blocking and tackling rather than significant innovation. Domino's experienced increases in revenue and operating profit of 18% and 28%, respectively, in the first quarter of 2010 after communicating in its advertising that it was responding to consumer dissatisfaction with its pizza recipe with an improved product.[4] Similarly, Microsoft's notorious reputation of a controlling, complex, and unreliable operating system was softened by the introduction of Windows 7, which was developed with advertising in which users explained how the new operating system integrated their ideas for improvement.[5] Finally, Hyundai is an excellent example of a firm once characterized by significant disequity that has substantially improved its position. In a difficult 2009 market for the auto industry, Hyundai increased sales over 6% in the United States, improving market share to 4.3% from 3.0% in 2008 with substantive changes in car design, warranty, and platform integration to improve cycle time.[6] Figure 6.4 illustrates Hyundai's desired shift on the industry's value map, particularly with a focus on new, more elegant car designs.

Clarifying Customer Perceptions

A significant insight in 3-Circle growth analysis is that items that emerge in Area E that are misperceptions can be corrected through communications. We would not claim to be the first to discover certain types of misperception in the marketplace that can be corrected. A clever example of this is *Rolling Stone* magazine's classic "perception vs. reality" ad campaign back in the 1980s and 1990s, which sought to correct major advertisers' misperception that the magazine's readership was composed primarily of hippies. The ads were two full pages—a left-hand page titled "perception" and a right-hand page titled "reality," each presenting insights about *previous* vs. *new* readers, respectively. One of the best-known versions of the ad had a left-hand page showing a peace sign, and a right-hand page showing a Mercedes-Benz hood ornament. Similarly,

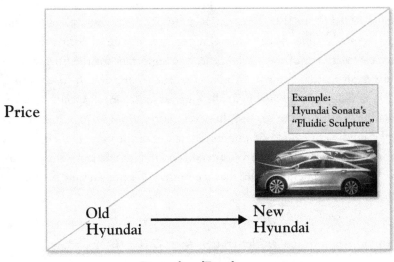

Figure 6.4. *Hyundai Sonata's "fluidic sculpture" value map repositioning.*

SC Johnson currently fends off the longtime perception for its Pledge furniture cleaner product that it leaves wax build-up by pointing out that the product does not even *have* wax in it! (The tag line is "No wax. No build-up.") Surprises in customer perceptions are a very common outcome in 3-Circle growth strategy projects, producing significant growth opportunities. We will detail a pharmaceutical case in chapter 9 in which the firm discovered and responded to important physician misperceptions about their drug's outcomes and managed care system.

Growth Imperative 2: Solidify and Update Area B (Points of Parity)

Points of parity are those dimensions of value that your offering is expected to have. Laptop computers have at minimum 3 or 4 gigabytes of hard drive space and 32 megabytes of RAM. Those basic requirements used to be a lot lower. The Wikipedia entry for Moore's Law (which describes the exponential growth of digital device capabilities) indicates that hard drive memory capacity—a standard feature of personal computers—grew from 0.01 gigabytes in 1985 to 1,000 gigabytes in 2010.[7] The issue here is that even points of parity evolve and move. Returning to the six lessons about attributes from chapter 4, there is a dynamic pattern to value creation in markets that begins with a firm's incentive to try something new—a new value-added feature like a camera on a cell phone, for example. Once the market finds value in that feature, it becomes a point of parity, that is, a basic expectation of the market. But it is important for the firm to keep an eye on that, as some firms may continue to improve it, for example, by improving picture quality or allowing for more video capacity or easier sharing. This is not to suggest that every effort to improve points of parity should be imitated without consideration of the value that customers obtain from it. Instead, the more general point is to take a systematic look at Area B attributes to ensure that your offering is not slipping behind on these table stakes.

Growth Imperative 3: Neutralize Area C (C→B or C→A)

In the normal course of competition in the free market, one of the most fundamental principles is that successful offerings get imitated unless they are protected legally or by unique resources, capabilities, and assets.

McDonald's has experienced success in mimicking both the higher quality coffee and, to some extent, the consumption experience of Starbucks stores, at substantially lower prices. McDonald's marketing communications program includes a billboard with huge lettering saying "four bucks is *dumb*," with a parenthetical remark below ("now serving espresso") and the golden arches logo in the lower right. Ironically, a McDonald's competitor has similarly pursued an imitation strategy so extreme that they depict a brazen Burger King (with the smiling plastic mask) breaking into McDonald's corporate headquarters to steal the secret plans for the Sausage McMuffin. Burger King wants you to know that you get the *exact* same product, with one difference: a price of $1.00 rather than $1.99. Each of these actions would be seeking to directly position south of the competitor on the value map, essentially with a denominator (price) strategy. We might think of three strategies related to neutralizing Area C:

- *Equal value: Match the competitors' benefits simply to neutralize them as a unique advantage.* Strategies that seek to neutralize Area C may be such strategies in which the firm seeks to turn the competitor's Area C attributes (their points of difference) into Area B attributes (points of parity). For example, Verizon has been very aggressive about promoting the superiority of its mobile phone coverage, with a campaign built around the strength of its coverage map relative to AT&T's. In a fierce advertising battle, AT&T responded in kind for a time, seeking to make coverage an Area B item. In addition, AT&T spent $2 billion improving its network in 2010. There was some measure of success in the campaign, as AT&T picked up new users, although it appears that those gains came from smaller carriers like Sprint and T-Mobile rather than Verizon.[8] Note that while the strategy of equalizing value on particular attributes does not create a superior advantage—it removes a reason for not choosing a brand, which can have a powerful effect on customer choices.
- *Better value.* A firm may instead seek to leapfrog a competitor on value. One way of doing this is to *match the competitor's Area C benefits, but at a lower price.* This is illustrated by Burger King's blatant, humorous effort to literally duplicate the

McDonald's breakfast sandwich, but to offer it at a significantly lower price (again, a *due south* positioning strategy on the value map). Alternatively, the firm might neutralize the competitor's advantage by developing *superior benefits at the same price* (a *due east* strategy). Eastern strategies would tend to involve the addition of value-added products or services that competitors do not, or cannot, offer. Examples of this would include the Infiniti with the "Around View Monitor" with cameras on all sides of the car, the Motorola-Verizon Droid surpassing the Apple-AT&T iPhone's features at a similar price, the computer manufacturer with a superior warranty, or the consumer-products firm that adds 30% more product volume in the package than the competitor but at the same price.

- *Live and let live.* While we may see prospects for improving customer value and choice in neutralizing the competitor's Area C, the larger assessment, in fact, should be whether or not the benefits of such a strategy exceed the costs for the firm. There may be Area C advantages that naturally belong to the competitor and would be too costly to try to match. For example, recall in chapter 2 that while standardized testing was a cost-feasible addition for Glenview New Church School (and a competitive must-have), it would be very difficult and costly for Glenview New Church to attempt to imitate the public school's broad curriculum (beyond the core). It is important that a cost-benefit analysis be applied in a disciplined way to match or imitate a competitor's advantages. Criteria for evaluating the desirability of such imitation would include not only investment and likely return financially but also the fit of the move with current positioning and strategy and the likelihood of provoking competitive reaction. For the market-share leader, a move to imitate a smaller underdog's actions may simply bring more attention to the underdog.

Growth Imperative 4: Reduce or Eliminate Nonvalued Benefits

Kim and Mauborgne's (2005) empirical research on value innovation and blue ocean strategy revealed an important element of strategy that had not been discussed previously. They found firms who were able to find growth, even in highly competitive industries, by reducing or even eliminating attributes or benefits that customers valued less, and by investing in significantly improving the most important values. An example is adapted in Figure 6.5, depicting the strategy for Quicken's personal finance software, which was introduced into an existing market of 42 powerful, but very complex and difficult-to-use, software products. Scott Cook, founder of Intuit, considered those products but also had in mind positioning against the simplest of all financial management products— the pencil! As Figure 6.5a shows, Quicken's value was in its ease of use but equivalent power relative to the software packages of the day, yet it maintained the speed and accuracy advantages over the pencil. The company simplified the product by stripping out many complex features and using straightforward language. The simpler product also costs less, illustrating the core principle in Kim and Mauborgne's (2005) concept of "value innovation"—that companies create significant gains in value by focusing on building a few benefits that customers value and eliminating or reducing those that are less valued. The elimination of some benefits can lower costs, leading to lower prices as well. Figure 6.5b illustrates the same Quicken positioning strategy as captured in a value map.

Growth Imperative 5: Build and Defend Area A

The 3-Circle model provides a simple way to explain the essence of competitive strategy: the goal is to build Area A relative to Area C. Seeking to shrink Area C may be part of that strategy. But building Area A is a code word for the raison d'être for any business—what truly unique value do you bring into the world? Having analyzed customer value and categorized the value using the seven categories in the framework, you will find a variety of ways to think about how to build the distinctive value in Area A. As captured in Table 6.3, there are a number of areas in the 3-Circle model that provide sources of value on which Area A might be built.

Quicken's innovation enhanced benefits by improving ease of use and removing complexity, and lowering cost.

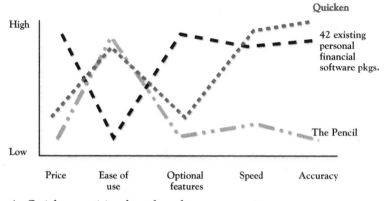

A. Quicken position based on features

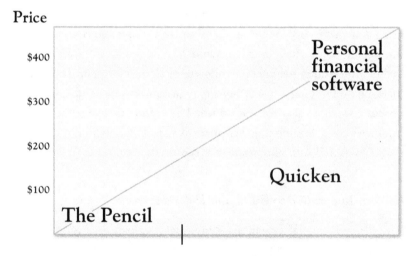

Benefits/Performance

B. Quicken position in a value map.

Figure 6.5. Quicken's innovation: Reducing complexity.

Source: Adapted from "Creating New Market Space," by W. C. Kim and R. Mauborgne, 1999, *Harvard Business Review* (January–February), 83–93.

Table 6.3. Growth Imperative 5: Building Area A

Growth strategy imperative	Question summary	Case examples
5. Build/expand Area A		
(i) Area B →Area A	• What points of parity might be built upon to enhance Area A?	• JetBlue
(ii) Area D →Area A	• Are there attributes that have become unimportant to customers that still may have some life in them? Can we connect them to the customer's value proposition?	• Kmart layaway • Key Bank—unbanked
(iii) Area E →Area A	• What disequities or potential equities might be improved to provide value beyond that of current competitors?	• Teflon • Tang • Ipana Toothpaste • Vionnet and Marimekko • Signode
(iv) Area F →Area A	• What competitor deficiencies might be exploited, at least short term, to create differential advantage?	• Southwest Airlines, baggage
(v) Area G →Area A	• What are the real drivers of demand for the products/services we make? • What are the deeper unmet needs for which new product and service solutions might be developed?	• Gain Detergent • Crocs shoes • David, Inc.

Ratchet Up Points of Parity (Area B→Area A)

JetBlue was founded on a unique passenger experience. Building upon the original model of Southwest Airlines of a regional hub-to-hub airline with an emphasis on low cost, JetBlue captured significant unique dimensions of value by taking a standard flying experience and enhancing the comfort and excitement of the passenger experience. In one of its early advertisements—a humorous "mockumentary"—JetBlue employees explain, for a variety of basic services, that when customers ask them to do something (e.g., seat them together with another passenger), they actually do it. So when a passenger asked for some headphones, "I hooked him up," notes a flight attendant. This is a parody on the notion that many existing airlines often fail to meet the most basic of expected services. Yet JetBlue's distinctive value is in taking a commoditized in-flight experience and significantly improving it. The firm seeks a very passenger-oriented in-flight experience from its attendants, and has both comfortable leather seats and entertainment systems for every passenger on every flight. This is a classic illustration of taking standard attributes in the overall value proposition and pushing them to new value-enhancing levels in ways that require significant investment. For such a strategy to work, the attributes or benefits must be (a) fundamentally important to customers, and (b) credibly differentiable among competitors. In certain circumstances, there may be opportunities for differentiation because an industry (both firms *and* customers) has become so accustomed to its points of parity that all take certain levels of value as given. So when Wal-Mart takes its standard in-store layout that has been virtually the same (and similar to other mass-merchant rivals) for decades and enhances colors, layout, and fashion orientation, the result is a remarkable contrast that sharpens the value customers obtain from its low-price Area A. In sum, raising the levels of Area B attributes to enhance Area A is often a process of exploring the customer's experience around existing attributes and then uncovering how to build a new experience.

Find Value in Old Ideas That Worked at One Time (Area D → Area A)

If we classify an attribute or benefit in Area D, it means that this dimension of value is or was jointly produced by each firm but that it is outside the customer's circle. It is possible that there still exists value in such retired attributes. Determining whether there might be value there, though, requires some skill in discrimination. There are examples of bringing back values that have been successful, as in car companies bringing back vintage cars or introducing classic design elements in contemporary cars. We might think of a category of value that may have seemed to go out of style but, in fact, is classic enough to have an appeal to certain consumers in every generation—for example, the simplicity and elegance of Frank Lloyd Wright architecture. Kmart created a point of difference by bringing back a layaway capability when difficult economic times set in back in 2008, and it got a great deal of positive press as a result. In a 2008 *Wall Street Journal* article, Mark Snyder, Kmart's chief marketing officer, noted, "While not sexy, layaway became the big idea at Kmart these holidays."[9] Similarly, in large banks, check cashing has not been a highly demanded service, as consumers typically deposit checks and electronic deposits have become increasingly common. As competition for middle-class and wealthy consumers has heated up, some banks have looked for business elsewhere, discovering a very large segment of "unbanked" or "underbanked" consumers who do not have relationships with banks, yet spend over $11 billion per year at financial institutions that cash checks.[10] In response, Key Bank has experimented with check-cashing services in a variety of retail bank branches, with specific technology for identifying customers and providing other services for a cash economy in which many customers engage.

Find Hidden Equity in Area E (Area E→Area A)

As noted earlier, there are multiple interpretations of Area E. The first we addressed previously: There are some dimensions of value that may be important and on which we are not meeting expectations. The strategy for such dimensions is to correct obvious problems to negate the disadvantage (a high priority). But the other, more subtle element of Area E (same with D and F) is that it may contain dimensions of value that are currently undervalued by the market. A couple of examples have been mentioned throughout this book. Upon first introduction, the feature "Teflon coated" was quickly relegated to Area E status, as consumers did not connect with the value of fat-free cooking, as the original promotion held. Yet when the feature was connected to a more important value (ease of clean-up, time savings), Teflon coating became an instant strong point of difference. Similarly, earlier we mentioned Tang's rise to prominence in Asia and other locations as the firm has leveraged the brand's recognition with packaging innovations that better connected with customer needs.

The general notion here is that the firm may discover in Area E hidden assets that may—with a little extra effort—connect well to customer values. In a classic *Harvard Business Review* article, Nariman Dhalla and

Sonia Yuspeh cite many examples of firms who gave up on certain brand assets under the assumption that they were in the mature phase of the product life cycle.[11] They cite the case of Ipana toothpaste, for example, given up for dead by its corporate parent and sold off to small investors. The new owners subsequently produced healthy sales for a reformulated product with the same packaging and branding, with later research showing 1.5 million regional users of the brand. More recent examples of the same phenomenon have occurred in fashion, with the successful reintroduction of the brands Vionnet and Marimekko, each long-ago pioneers in the industry and now experiencing new energy through new ownership.[12]

At times, an organization may not realize the strength of its current offering. In the earlier cited work on decommoditization, Rangen and Bowman offer up the example of Signode Corporation, a manufacturer of steel strapping for industrial applications.[13] In customer research, the company discovered that a certain segment of customers put a high value on its bundled offering of strapping equipment, supplies, and engineering service. Essentially, the unique value of the bundling was unknown to the firm, who assumed it was unimportant in the customer's decision calculus. In the firm's assessment (prior to the research), this was essentially an Area E item, not believed to be particularly influential in customer decisions. The discovery that this was more important to some customer segments than first thought led to clearer segmentation of the market and more profitable pricing policies.

Exploit the Competition's Weakness (Area F→Area A)

As noted earlier, there are risks associated with attacking a competitor on a weakness and potentially leveraging that weakness into a strength or point of difference. However, the strategy may be most likely undertaken when the competitor will find it difficult or unprofitable to follow. A recent illustration is Southwest Airline's taking advantage of the baggage fees introduced by legacy airlines like United, Delta, and Continental. Southwest has countered this move with a steadfast refusal to introduce fees for the first two bags checked and a humorous advertising campaign built around the theme "Bags Fly Free." While debate has ensued about Southwest's decision to eschew significant revenue the other airlines are gathering, the company points to its gains in passenger miles and load factor, each surprisingly up 9% and 11%, respectively, in August 2009.[14] Southwest executive Kevin Krone reflects the company's resolve to stick with the no fee policy, noting, "If we're trying to get people to travel, we should probably let people take their suitcase."

Explore and Leverage the White Space (Area G →Area A)

One of the exciting dimensions of the 3-Circle model is the fact that it graphically illustrates a reality that we often lose sight of on a day-to-day basis: that customers always have unmet needs or needs that have not been fully met. In the nearly $7-billion laundry detergent market, Procter & Gamble (P&G) was able to make significant strides in market share for their brand Gain, originally introduced in 1969 as an enzyme-driven laundry soap for difficult stains. More recently, deeper study of consumer needs uncovered a powerful—if somewhat obvious in hindsight—conclusion that consumers are driven in laundry detergent choice as much by what they *smell* as by how the detergent cleans. In fact, scent connected especially well for ethnic segments, such as Hispanics.[15] The repositioning of the brand around scent was enormously successful, as Gain picked up 3 percentage points in market share, that increment valued at $198 million annually, and the brand became P&G's 23rd billion-dollar brand. In a similar vein, Crocs shoes had to counter long-standing disequity that its shoes were ugly by bringing attention to the *comfort* of the shoes with the theme "feel the love" (see Figure 6.6). Croc's revenue increased 24% in the 1st quarter of 2010, compared to the 2009 results, with a $28-million improvement in net income.[16]

In each of these cases, the firms did not discover needs that they were not already aware of. What is different here is that once the firms understood the importance of these values, in each case, they asked how they could more effectively deliver on or connect with these needs. In short, these efforts were not framed as technology in search of markets but instead were understood to be *customer needs in search of solutions*. That is a very important distinction.

The topic of brainstorming around unmet needs is quite important (and complex), and there exist a number of helpful sources that dive deeply into the topic.[17] It is beyond the scope of the current work to

Figure 6.6. Crocs advertisement.

overview these approaches, but we will offer a short, concrete insight that builds upon our earlier coverage of understanding deeper *customer values*. Consider a firm we will call David, Inc., which competes in electronic commerce industry, working with billion-dollar customers in a targeted industry. The competitor is Goliath Corp., inventor of the current technology used in the industry. Our analyst for David, Inc. (let us call him Dave), undertook a 3-Circle growth strategy analysis with a strong predisposition that to win business from Goliath, it would be critical to reduce and allocate the customers' costs for them, to be compliant with security protocols and governance practices, and to reduce complexity and time. While these expectations are all accurate at a certain level, in-depth interviews with customers had an eye-opening impact on Dave's thinking:

> So, what did we learn in talking to customers? A LOT. News flash—analysts write about features and capabilities, not customer needs. If you want to find out what is really going on, ask a customer—they are happy to tell you . . . I thought it was all about technology and

capabilities. Sure, technology is important, but what customers are really looking for is partnership.

Prospective customers ultimately conveyed, very frankly, that they were tired of being treated like a "captive audience" by Goliath Corp. Frustration was such that when one vice president of finance for a potential customer was asked, "What matters most in a technology vendor?" she replied, "The ability to easily replace them." A vice president of information technology (IT) unexpectedly answered the same question, "The ability to help us move faster." Rather than being concerned about *features* offered by a vendor, he was ultimately concerned with the fact that *his reputation* was on the line in getting the IT infrastructure to a point where it could keep up with, and not constrain, the speed with which his firm was doing business. These deeper Area G insights and frustrations gave the David, Inc., team new inspiration. Instead of being frustrated by the impossible task of unseating the dominant competitor, the team developed strategy with the belief that there were ways to quietly and effectively partner with customers. Business could be taken from Goliath Corp. not as a pure cost-reduction positioning (although that was important), but more broadly in terms of moving quickly to next-generation solutions and to broaden the types of information that could be electronically moved in the interest of partnering and helping customers maintain the pace of business.

Chapter Summary

Let us summarize the chapter's key concepts by returning to the Kindle example from chapter 5. What are the implications of the growth strategy framework for Kindle's possible outlets for growth? We can get some initial speculative insight—subject, of course, to the need for additional research.

- *Kindle's Area A*: Kindle's positioning as a dedicated electronic reader is very clear, as it was essentially the pioneer. Its features build to the core benefits of focused reading and undistracted immersion, as well as inexpensive access to books.

- *Imperative 1: Correct deficiencies.* There may be some borderline deficiencies here, particularly related to navigation. While the system moves relatively quickly, the difficulty of using the tiny joystick can be frustrating both in terms of speed and accuracy of navigation.
- *Imperative 2: Solidify and update Area B.* If book selection is currently roughly equivalent (and limited) between Kindle and iPad, then this may be an area we can expect differences to emerge because it is both important to customers and a function of building and shifting partnerships with publishers, which could quickly add access.
- *Imperative 3: Neutralize Area C.* There is, of course, some overlap here with Imperative 1. We designated navigation as more of a deficiency because it has an immediate, potentially dissatisfying effect in simple operation of the device. Related, but perhaps not as immediately urgent, is the availability of touchscreen technology and color. The point here is not simply to mimic the iPad but to enable design changes that will improve the user experience for the focused purpose. It is conceivable that no changes should be made regarding the Kindle navigation if most users perceive minimal effects on the user experience or if such changes reduced the speed of the device.
- *Imperative 4: Reduce and eliminate nonvalue.* Since the Kindle is already believed to have value because of its simplicity and single purpose, it is fair to suggest that there may be few areas in which to reduce the reading-focused capability. However, it is important to note the mantra of "keeping Kindle simple" is strategically very important, as there may be temptation to gravitate toward greater capability.[18]
- *Imperative 5: Build and expand Area A.* To be selective here, we will focus on an Area G item that is important to readers, particular on niche genres or topics. Collectively, readers demand a large book selection. Currently, each competitor in the eReader market is limited to a select number of publishing relationships. Blogger Damon Brown (cf. note 16) offers the following advice:

There are hundreds of medium-sized (or smaller) publishers available within and outside of the United States. Amazon wisely is going after the smaller guys, too, with its recent royalty (and rights!) heavy contract option appealing to self-publishers, a group Apple didn't acknowledge (during a keynote address).

The development of reading-related applications and more extensive study, which allowed the sizing of benefit and interest segments in the reading market, could be important vehicles for reaching readers more effectively than Apple does.

The importance of the 3-Circle framework is that it allows a systematic walk-through of the dimensions of value currently available on the market and a rigorous review of growth strategy questions with emphasis on all the important value dimensions in the market (but current, known dimensions and those not so well known). The goal is to stay focused on how our organization might build a unique position by developing important value for customers that competitors cannot match. A critical issue in this is the notion of capability—once we develop ideas for building growth strategy, how do we execute them? Capabilities, resources, and assets are the focus of the next chapter.

CHAPTER 7

Implementation

An Inside View of the Organization

In the Studebaker National Museum sits an automobile that is powered by ion beams. Engineers within the Studebaker Corporation saw an opportunity to build an automobile that used a completely revolutionary design and energy source. They built a prototype of the automobile but lacked the capabilities and assets to produce the ion beams to propel the car as they had planned. If it were possible to produce the envisioned automobile, it would have produced a solid Area A, a point of difference, in the automotive industry. Because they were unable to deliver on their strategy, their prototype sits in the Studebaker National Museum as another good idea that lacked the resources, capabilities, and assets necessary to make it work. The Studebaker Company had the vision but lacked the internal resources, capabilities, and assets to bring their idea to life. The world is full of executives and entrepreneurs who have tremendous strategies and sensational ideas, but who are unable to execute those strategies or carry out those ideas to realize the anticipated dream.

What is in a company's DNA, its internal characteristics, that makes it possible to produce the goods and services desired by the customer? What are the characteristics that both build and sustain an organization's current competitive advantage (Area A) and have the potential to create future advantages?

Having identified areas of customer need and opportunity to build a sustainable point of difference, an Area A, executives face the daunting task of implementation. This requires them to look for the resources, capabilities, and assets necessary to successfully achieve Area A. Sometimes the necessary resources, capabilities, and assets can be found inside the firm; other times, the executive must look outside the firm.

Da Ali G Show is a satirical TV series starring Sacha Baron Cohen. During its second season, Cohen, playing the lead character "Ali G," carried out comedic interviews with unsuspecting celebrities and professionals. In one episode, Ali visited with an investor and showed a blank skateboard, without wheels, and introduced it as a "hoverboard." Ali explained that he had seen it in a movie (*Back to the Future*) years ago, and so he knew it was possible to produce one and that it would have huge market potential. In fact, Ali explained he was amazed that someone had not already produced the hoverboard since it had already been in the movies. He went on to explain that all he needed from the investor was a team of scientists with the technology, knowledge, and skills to make the hoverboard work.[1] Ali G had a great idea, with a potentially huge Area A—teens would have lined up to get their own hoverboard; the only thing lacking was the back office, inside resources, capabilities, and assets necessary to make it happen!

Customers rarely know anything about what occurs inside an organization, much less care about what an organization must do to create the attributes they desire. They are often completely unaware of what it takes in terms of the skills, resources, or costs necessary to make attributes and features they desire possible. In most cases, customers only care about the desired benefits that are salient to them are delivered in a cost-effective, efficient manner. For example, most computer users do not understand the internal design and associated knowledge and skills required to create a product with the attributes they desire. In fact, customers will often call those involved with the internal workings of the computer "nerds" or "geeks," especially when they enthusiastically try to explain the internal beauty of the machine and the competencies involved! Most customers only see the computer's attributes and expect a great product for a great price. Yet the inside resources, capabilities, and assets necessary for the production of a computer not only makes the current attributes available but also makes future attributes and cost saving possible. The link between the company's DNA and desired customer attributes can be graphically demonstrated as follow:

Internal Resources   →   Customer attributes/benefits →
Capabilities & Assets →   Position

Because of the link between inside company resources, assets, and capabilities necessary to deliver the attributes customer demand, it is essential that company executives have a clear understanding of not only what organizational DNA is used to deliver current customer attributes and benefits but also how it might be used to deliver future attributes and benefits. Executives who become so focused on current internal practices and characteristics necessary to deliver attributes that current customers demand, without keeping an eye on attributes that future customers will desire, risk market myopia that will make his or her firm irrelevant over time.[2] This chapter is designed to help you understand the essential internal building blocks of execution and how to locate them. In the process, you will discover the essential value drivers necessary for your organization to have a sustainable competitive advantage.

Looking Inside the 3 Circles for the Building Blocks of Product Attributes and Service

In chapter 6, we described growth strategies. It is now essential that we look inside the firm to determine whether the building blocks exist to actually execute the strategy. Naturally, executives look inside their organizations for the internal resources or building blocks that form the strategic bundles necessary to execute strategies to build their points of differences, or, their Area A. These building blocks are the input that managers use to create product and service attributes that meet current and future customer needs and bring the firm a competitive advantage.[3] In this book, we have simply collectively referred to those internal building blocks as the internal resources, capabilities, and assets of the organization that may or may not be known to the customer who could only be familiar with the more visible attributes of the product or service. Rigsby and Greco described financial, physical, human, technological, and reputation resources as the major internal firm assets necessary for executing strategy (see Table 7.1).[4]

Resources, capabilities, and assets are both tangible and intangible and are tied either permanently or semipermanently to the organization.[5] For example, employees in the organization provide key capabilities and competencies to the organization. Such capabilities and competencies are intangible and consist of the knowledge, skills, thought patterns, motivation, culture, and networks of the employees in the organization.[6] Dubois and Rothwell argued that employee capabilities could be further classified

Table 7.1. Firm Resources

Resource	Main characteristic	Key indicator
Financial resources	• The firm's borrowing capacity and its internal funds generation determine its investment capacity and its cyclical resilience.	• Debt/equity ratio • Ratio of net cash to capital expenditure • Credit rating
Physical resources	• The size, location, technical sophistication, and flexibility of plant and equipment; location and alternative uses for land and buildings, and reserves of raw materials constrain the firm's set of production possibilities and determine the potential for cost and quality advantage.	• Resale values of fixed assets • Vintage of capital equipment • Scale of plants • Alternative uses of fixed assets
Human resources	• The training and expertise of employees determine the skills available to the firm. The adaptability of employees determines the strategic flexibility of the firm. The commitment and loyalty of the employees determine the firm's ability to maintain competitive advantage.	• Educational, technical, professional qualifications of employees • Pay rates relative to industry average
Technological resources	• Stock of technology including proprietary technology (patents, copyrights, trade secrets) and expertise in its application of know-how. Resources for innovation: research facilities, technical and scientific employees.	• Number and significance of patents • Revenue from patent licenses • R&D staff as a percentage of total employees
Reputation	• Reputation with customers through the ownership of brands, established relationships with customers, the association of the firm's products with quality, reliability, and so on. The reputation of the company with the suppliers of components, finance, labor services, and other inputs.	• Brand recognition • Price premium over competing brands • Percentage of repeat buying • Objective measures of product performance • Level and consistency of company performance

Source: Adapted from Rigsby, J. and Greco, G. (2003), Mastering Strategy. New York, NY: McGraw Hill.

as either technical-functional or personal functioning.[7] Technical capabilities include specialized knowledge, skills, and capabilities that can be used in particular ways within the company. For example, gas metal arc welders have specialized skills because of their ability to weld aluminum at Boeing. Without this capability, Boeing would be unable to deliver fabrication attributes that its airframe customers value. Likewise, computer programmers at Microsoft and Apple have specialized capabilities necessary to produce attributes that end users value in their computer operating systems. A second category of human resource competencies is "personal" and includes management skills, strategic views, networking abilities, and psychological characteristics. Southwest Airlines has often been cited for its managerial skills that create customer relationship attributes that are valued by customers. These managerial competencies have helped build attributes in Southwest Airline's Area A that other airlines have not been able to imitate. While technical competencies are easier to define, interpret, and apply than personal competencies, personal competencies are also very important and cannot be overlooked.[8]

Finances, plants, equipment, and physical assets are resources that are absolutely necessary for creation of attributes that are both valued and expected by customers. Physical resources also include the intellectual property and trade secrets that can be used to create and sustain an Area-A market advantage. Distinctive patents, copyrights, and other assets protect the organization's advantage from being imitated by competitors and make an important feature of the resource bundle that sustains the distinctiveness of competencies. Physical resources are not considered firm competencies; however, they are necessary for the human competencies to create products and services that are valued by customers. An organization can have the best human capital and capabilities in the industry, but if the organization lacks the resources to execute those competencies, it cannot build its competitive advantage. Likewise, a company can have all the distinctive physical resources but lack the core competencies necessary to develop the products valued by customers for a distinctive advantage. For example, the University of Iowa built a laser-technology building with distinctive, state-of-the-art equipment; however, the university was unable to attract key scientists with the core competencies necessary to bring the university an Area A in laser research. As a result, the building was renamed the "Iowa Advanced Technology Laboratories" and now houses multidisciplinary research rather than the planned laser technology focus.[9] A primary reason new ideas and ventures fail is that they lack the bridge funding and physical resources necessary to bundle with human competencies to deliver a product or service to the market. Without the distinctive physical resources to complement the human competencies (knowledge, capabilities, and skills), the organization cannot successfully produce attributes that bring the organization a sustainable advantage.

These resources, capabilities, and assets are structured to build the attributes that are viewed by customers. The sequence of activities that an organization develops to produce attributes often defines the firm, its processes, and culture. Figure 7.1 graphically demonstrates how resources, capabilities, and assets might work together to produce attributes, products, and services.

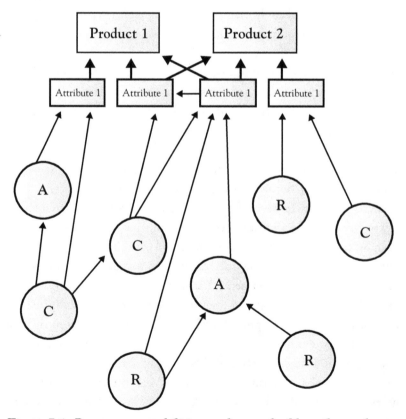

Figure 7.1. Resources, capabilities, and assets build attributes that differentiate products.

How the resources, capabilities, and assets are deployed and associated is an essential characteristic of the organization. As described previously, Southwest Airlines may have human and physical resources similar to any other airline—the way they link the resources and skills to produce the customer-valued attributes is distinctive, giving them a competitive advantage. Michael Porter described how the airline's attributes are structured in a way that brings the airline a competitive advantage based on low cost and a reputation as the fun airline (Figure 7.2); however, the figure fails to demonstrate the inside view, that is, the competencies and physical resource chains that underlie the attributes.[10] For example, Southwest Airlines has mechanics whose competencies specialize in the maintenance of a single physical resource—the Boeing 737 airplane. They do not have human competencies in meal preparation or boarding-pass production and distribution and associated physical assets. Southwest has linked the human competencies and the necessary physical resources in such a way that the value chain itself—the way the resources and competencies are bundled—gives Southwest Airlines a distinctive position in the industry, that is, a very strong and sustainable Area A. It must also be noted that the

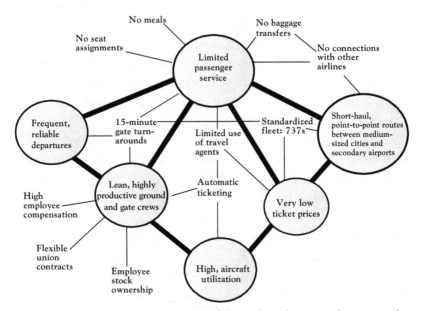

Figure 7.2. Southwest Airlines attribute value chains and connected activities.

Source: Adapted from "What is Strategy?" by M. Porter, 1998, in *The Strategy Reader*, ed. S. Segal-Horn, pp. 73–99, Malden, MA: Blackwell.

competencies and resources employed by Southwest Airlines are tightly focused, and those not fitting their business model are closely examined to determine whether they can be developed in some way to grow the company or whether they should simply be eliminated to reduce costs.

It is critical that management understand how resource, capability, and asset competencies are bundled to create and grow Area A and sustain Area B for their organization. The DNA of any firm lies in how building blocks such as employee skills, knowledge, and capabilities—often called competencies—as well as its physical resources, assets, and networks fit together to form a unique strategic bundle.[11] Strategic bundles are aggregations of the firm's internal attributes (skills, capabilities, knowledge), often invisible to the market, which have the potential of meeting current and future customer needs and values. For a bundle to be "core" to the business it must contribute to its long-term prosperity and be a source of competitive advantage; the bundle is the DNA that makes it possible for the firm to have a viable, sustainable Area A in the 3-Circle model.

Typically, both the firm and its competition have resources that are distinctive. These are areas E and F (see Figure 7.4). There is also an area of overlap in which both the competitor and the firm have resources, capabilities, and assets that are common; this can be considered a point of internal similarity. Resources that form internal similarity are often the ones necessary to produce the attributes populating Area B. In commodity markets, the area of internal similarity may be very large as competitors imitate each other (restaurants) or are highly regulated to be similar (banking). This is shown in Area B of Figure 7.4.

Building blocks (resources, capabilities, networks, knowledge, assets) in areas E and D do not fall within the customer circle and are therefore more difficult to associate directly to the firm's current revenues stream associated with Area A or Area B.[12] Area E and D resources, capabilities, and assets may play an indirect, noncritical role in producing the attributes currently valued by the customer, but we cannot conclude that they have no value. As shown in chapter 6, Area E building blocks may or may not be currently used in a strategic bundle, but they have potential for building Area A by addressing an unmet customer need found in Area G or imitating a competitor's advantage found in Area C. Simply because internal building blocks in Area E may not currently play a direct role in creating Area A or B customer value, they still may have potential. Likewise, it was also shown in chapter 6 that even Area D resources, capabilities, and assets can be resurrected and can create or strengthen Areas A and B.

Adding the customer circle to Figure 7.4 allows us to examine all of the resources underlying both the firm and the competition's ability to produce current and future products and attributes. Figure 7.4 is a representation of the entire 3-Circle model from the inside view. The inside view of all of the areas of the 3-Circle model pertaining to the firm can be described as follows:

- *Area A.* This area includes resource bundles necessary to produce attributes that are valued by customers by meeting real needs. The unique combination of employee competencies, knowledge, and company assets gives the firm a competitive advantage in the market and competitors cannot easily imitate this (due to the tacitness of the knowledge, intellectual-property protection, scarce resources, and so on). Likewise, there are no close substitutes for the resource bundle that can produce product or service attributes that may satisfy the customer need in the same or similar way. To sustain this advantage, the firm must protect, and continually improve, the resource bundle to stay ahead of competitors who seek to imitate their attributes by producing better resource bundles (improved factors of production by cost, knowledge, skills, etc.). These resource bundles make it possible for the firm to produce attributes that bring the firm abnormal, above-industry average profits.
- *Area B.* This Area consists of resource bundles necessary to produce attributes that are valued by customers and meet real customer needs; however, these bundles are similar to those of competitors in the industry (as described in this chapter and shown in Figure 7.3). These resource bundles are necessary to produce the minimum attributes required by customers in the market. The factors of production making up these resource bundles are not unique and can be copied by others. While customers may value the attributes resulting from Area B resources, they only bring the firm normal, average profits. If there is a small or no Area A or C and there is a large Area B, the firm finds itself in a commodity market (as shown in

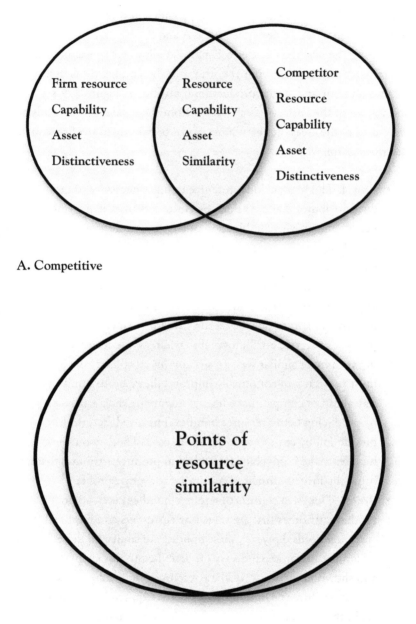

A. Competitive

B. Commodity

Figure 7.3. Firm and competitor internal perspective.

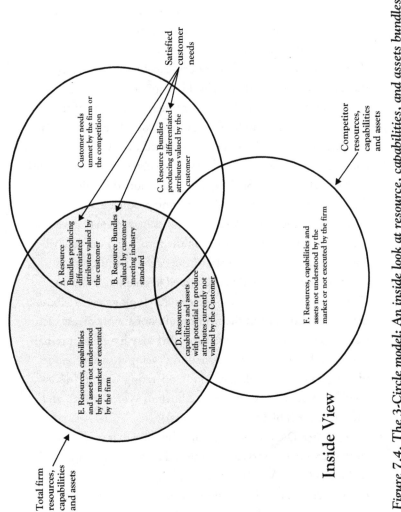

Satisfied
customer
needs

Customer needs
unmet by the firm or
the competition

C. Resource Bundles
producing differentiated
attributes valued by the
customer

Competitor
resources,
capabilities
and assets

A. Resource
Bundles producing
differentiated
attributes valued by
the customer

B. Resource Bundles
valued by customer
meeting industry
standard

F. Resources, capabilities and
assets not understood by the
market or not executed by the firm

E. Resources, capabilities
and assets not understood
by the market or executed
by the firm

D. Resources,
capabilities and assets
with potential to produce
attributes currently not
valued by the Customer

Total firm
resources,
capabilities
and assets

Inside View

Figure 7.4. The 3-Circle model: An inside look at resource, capabilities, and assets bundles.

Figure 7.3, Area B). Thus, firms face the constant struggle to find differentiated resource bundles and a competitive advantage. Yet to remain competitive, firms must maintain Area B competencies because they make possible the delivery of those minimal attributes required by customers of all organizations in industry. Failure to deliver Area B attributes both threatens the market relevance of the firm to the customer and gives the competitor an advantage.

- *Area E.* Area E consists of resources, capabilities, and assets that are either indirectly involved in supporting those that are used to build Area A and/or B attributes, or are part of the company's unused building-block inventory. These resources may include such things as employee skills, knowledge, and competencies as well as the firm's physical resources, assets, and intellectual property. Such resources are more difficult to tie directly to the firm's revenue generating product and service attributes. Some of the Area E resources may, or may never, provide customer value now or in the future and can safely be eliminated. Still, the potential of the Area E resource inventory must be considered (as described in chapters 5 and 6). The potential of Area E resources in developing new attributes may be substantial and the firm should not simply divest such resources without careful analysis. IBM may have had internal resources, but the company failed to develop microprocessors (developed by Motorola and Intel), operating systems (developed by Microsoft), software (the birth of WordPerfect), and chips (the birth of Texas Instruments).

- *Area D.* Area D consists of resource bundles that may have created product or service attributes that were valued by customers (areas A or B) but are no longer appreciated. Area D resources are not distinctive because the competition has similar resources with the same potential. Area D resources are a very difficult case. While they may be able to be used to develop Area A (as described earlier), the competitor is likely to follow. As a result, to sustain attributes, products, and services emerging from Area D, resources must be combined with others from Areas E, A, or B in ways that are rare, valuable, and nonsubstitutable in order to sustain customer value and the distinctiveness necessary to grow Area A. American automobile manufacturers have successfully reintroduced outdated models that customers no longer desired. For example, Chrysler brought back the retro-styled PT Cruiser (see Figure 7.5).

Customer demand for the PT Cruiser had waned, and the company stopped producing the car in the early 1950s. Today's customers would likely not value the features and attributes of the older model. To successfully reintroduce the PT Cruiser, Chrysler used resources, capabilities, and assets from areas E, A, and B to add features today's customers desire—from scalloped headlights, a chromed front grill, brake cooling ducts, and antilock brakes, to new audio systems, including an MP3 player jack and satellite radio, a turbocharged 2.4 L four-cylinder engine, and the latest in cruise control. Simply producing a Cruiser with the features from the classic 1940s model, exclusively using Area D resources and associated features, would have failed to penetrate the customer circle. The successful integration of current Area A, B, and E resources

Figure 7.5. Chrysler's retro PT Cruiser making areas D and A.

Source: http://www.new-cars.com/2003/chrysler/pt-cruiser/2003-chrysler-pt-cruiser-woodie.jpg

added desirable features to the PT Cruiser that led to the growth of Chrysler's Area A and the car's being recognized as *Motor Trend*'s car of the year in 2001.

Growing Area B by using Area D resources may be necessary to meet the new minimum market standards; however, because customers will expect the attributes of all companies in the market, demands for quality will be high and there will be downward price pressure. While it is necessary to maintain Area B market attributes, investing heavily in Area B may simply increase customer expectations and organizational costs without building profits. Thus, the profit-margin potential will be low. Thus, resources, capabilities, and assets found in Area D must be assessed with care.

The natural inclination is to eliminate resources, capabilities, and assets located in Area D because they burn valuable resources, have little discernable connection to the revenue-generating attributes of the firm, and, as a result, may be a fatal distraction to the central mission and vision of the company. Yet to remove those resources may give competitors an advantage because the firm can no longer pose the threat of retaliation through imitation. Firms retain these Area D resources because if they do not, competitors who also have them can build a competitive advantage unchallenged.[13] Still, as described here, unless the resources in Area D are transformed or bundled with other organizational resources, capabilities, and assets they have very little chance of building a meaningful advantage in a way that cannot be imitated by the competitor.

Growth From Resources, Capabilities, and Assets Inside the Company

The key challenge for management is to recognize internal capabilities, skills, resources, knowledge, networks, and so on that can be aggregated into bundles or competencies that can grow and sustain current value for the customers (Area A), have the potential of building new value by adding to Area A (E with potential for A), and must be maintained to deliver required attributes (Area B). While the resources within Area D may or may not be the type that will be appreciated and valued by customers, management must know them and make good decisions about what to do with them. Management must decide whether to remove or retain

Area D resources. They may decide to retain Area D resources because they believe, correctly or incorrectly, that their competitors may build an advantage if they do not, or they can reconfigure resources and grow Area A. Yet keeping those resources can be a distraction and add unnecessary costs to the firm. Such blocks may be obsolete resources (inventory), outdated skills, and equipment, and, yet, management still holds on for fear of what competitors with those same resources may do. Still, there is a chance that they may be correct in their perception, and so management tends to retain, and even protect, Area D resources.

A building block in Area E has the potential of having attributes capable of growing Area A and strengthening Area B. One of the primary jobs of management is to find, sustain, and skillfully aggregate internal building blocks of core competencies to produce attributes that can lead to a differentiated, sustainable advantage (equity) in terms of features or cost, offering a limited, but highly desirable, subset of attributes.

A strategic bundle consists of the core building blocks that have the potential of bringing a sustainable competitive advantage to the company. Strategic bundles have the potential of being rare and unique not only because of the building blocks (skills, abilities, and knowledge) but also because of the way they combined to form the bundles.[14] Competitors may be able to imitate an asset or a resource, but it is extremely difficult for them to imitate the way they are combined with knowledge, skills, and experience to form a strategic bundle. Likewise, there is no substitute for a firm's unique strategic bundle that creates product and service attributes valued by the customer.

Progressive Insurance

Recall from the opening chapter of this book the situation faced by Peter Lewis of Progressive Insurance as he developed growth strategy in the 1990s. Consumer dissatisfaction with automobile insurance companies was high, particularly regarding claims-processing times. As depicted in Figure 7.6, drilling down into this Area D disequity reveals its significance; it is ultimately connected to consumers' peace of mind, an important driver of human behavior, particularly in a context as stressful as automobile accidents. Also recall that Peter Lewis had lost a younger brother in an auto accident and so had a deep understanding of the

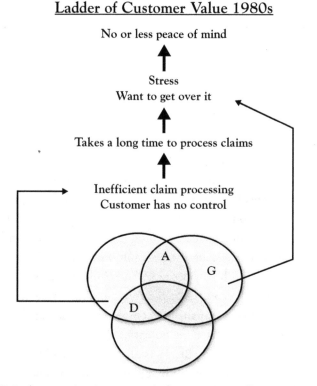

Figure 7.6. *Automotive insurance industry prior to Progressive transformation: An outside, customer view.*

emotional trauma caused by an accident. After sensing the level of consumer dissatisfaction with the industry upon California's passage of Proposition 103, which penalized the industry, Lewis reasoned that the most substantive way that Progressive could deliver value to customers was to create an "immediate response" capability that would dramatically reduce response times to auto accidents. Because this was born of real customer value and was very difficult to accomplish, it also had the potential to substantially differentiate Progressive from its competitors. But then the issue was how does a firm build such a capability?

Lewis set about developing strategies to deliver the peace of mind valued and desired by the market. He decided that a strategy of immediate response would deliver the distinctive value to bring this peace of mind and grow Area A. His strategy was to speed up claim processing in a more humane way that did not add to the trauma customers already suffered from the accident. To implement the strategy of a product with those service attributes, Lewis had to locate the resources, capabilities, and assets to successfully deliver the program. Attributes of the proposed program included an instant claims workbench, databases that were accurate and accessible to customers, committed and dedicated employees, and disciplined management. All of these proposed strategies and attributes are on the outside view of the 3-Circles model, viewed and appreciated by customers.

Next, Lewis had to determine whether he could implement his strategies and develop the required product and service attributes. This required Lewis to identify, develop, or acquire the internal resources, capabilities, and assets necessary to deliver the attribute and product value customers demanded that would bring peace of mind. He recognized that he would need radically different resources, assets, company culture, structure, and leadership to overcome the "high prices, bloated bureaucracies and poor service" characteristic of the industry.[15] His company shared the same skills, abilities, and technology as all other insurance companies. Lewis recognized that he needed a new resource bundle of resources, capabilities, and assets to deliver the value that customers desired. To provide immediate response, Lewis had to create an ultrafast, no-hassle, customer-friendly claims service. Internally, he had to develop an entirely new approach to human resources, including employees that were ready to serve customers 24 hours a day, 7 days a week. As Lewis put it, technology is not "worth a thing without topflight talent" and that they needed the "best people in the industry as measured by education, intelligence, initiative, work ethic and work record."[16] The immediate-response team needed an information system with software that could efficiently manage a very smooth information flow. Within Progressive's information-systems department, Lewis found competencies to develop software to enable the necessary concurrent information flow to make the service attributes that delivered the customer value. This information system has all the characteristics of a sustainable competitive advantage. The new information system and its management were necessary for implementing the information-transparency strategy. It also opened a sales channel for Progressive appreciated by customers and different from the exclusive direct sales approach utilized by other companies. While competitors have tried to imitate Progressive, "no other insurance company can instantly move information back and forth between a laptop and a mainframe and keep claims moving toward resolution."[17] Lewis found he needed to add new assets to his resource bundle to deliver the attributes necessary to meet customer needs, including laptop computers and immediate-response vehicles. In short, to meet the market need Lewis had identified, he needed to develop a resource bundle by looking both inside and outside Progressive, for the new resources, capabilities, and assets necessary to bring the peace of mind his clients desired. Figure 7.7 shows the internal view of Progressive and its competitors. Note that most of the distinctive, internal resources used to implement Lewis's strategies are not visible to the customers. They will see the product and service and their associated attributes; however, they may not have any idea of what Progressive does to deliver them.

Progressive developed new, distinctive resources, and capabilities to deliver immediate response

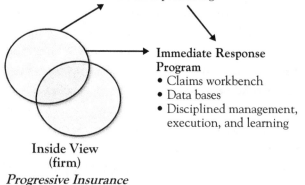

Distinctive INSIDE Resources:
- Human resources/culture
- Information system capabilities
- Technology development new software and web presence
- Human resource management
- Customer linking
- New accident logistics and claims processing

Immediate Response Program
- Claims workbench
- Data bases
- Disciplined management, execution, and learning

Inside View
(firm)
Progressive Insurance

Figure 7.7. Progressive: An inside view.

It is the inside resources, capabilities, and assets that brings Progressive its sustainable competitive advantage. Progressive's resource bundle consists of DNA that is valuable (it satisfies the client value of "peace of mind"); is rare (no other company has the resource bundle); cannot be copied (Progressive consistently stays ahead of its competition that consistently tries to imitate their bundle); and that has no close substitutes. In 1998, the industry as a whole had experienced 5 years of underwriting losses. During that same time period, Progressive had underwriting margins of over 8% and annual revenues in excess of $4 billion, up 36% from the previous year.[18] Recognizing the attributes that customers value and developing and capitalizing upon Progressive's resources, capabilities, and assets has helped the company develop and grow its distinctive advantage, that is, its Area A. Figure 7.8 shows the value ladder of the Progressive customers after its transformation. Progressive's internal resources enabled the company to deliver the attributes recognized by customers and bring them the peace of mind they desired.

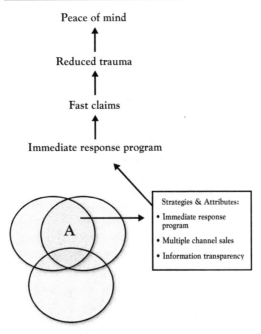

Current Ladder of Customer Value

Peace of mind

↑

Reduced trauma

↑

Fast claims

↑

Immediate response program

Strategies & Attributes:

• Immediate response program

• Multiple channel sales

• Information transparency

A

Figure 7.8. Automotive insurance industry after Progressive transformation: Outside customer view.

Chapter Summary

Whether the resources, capabilities, and assets—the firm's resource bundle—can be found inside the company, it is absolutely essential that the bundle is in place to properly execute your strategy and grow your competitive advantage. At times, your resource bundle is easily accessible. While this makes implementation easy, it also makes it easy for competitors to imitate your advantage and reduce it to a commodity-type offering (Area B). Arguably, your advantage is best sustained when you can develop a resource bundle that has the attributes of a competitive advantage—resources, capabilities, and assets that are rare, have value, and cannot be copied or substituted.

CHAPTER 8

The Dynamics of Customer Value and Competitive Advantage

Youngme Moon's new work, entitled *Different*, is an essay on differentiation in a competitive marketplace.[1] In the book, Moon recounts how, in her early teaching experience, she provided detailed feedback to students on their work on specific dimensions of performance relative to the class average. She identified an interesting and very natural tendency for students to stop developing areas in which they exceeded the class average and to instead focus on improving the areas in which they were below the class average. Moon notes, "The most creative thinkers in the room were intent on improving their analytical skills, while the most analytical thinkers in the room were intent on improving their creative contributions." The interesting outcome of these rational instincts is that the students in the class all tended to regress to the mean. That is, those who initially had unique advantages in certain areas did not develop those advantages but instead sought to become more like others on the dimensions in which they lagged.

Now consider this in extension to the competitive marketplace. Moon recounts, in simple fashion, the distinctive positions of Jeep and Nissan in the off-road vehicle market 20 years ago, when Jeep's point of difference was its reputation as a *rugged* sport utility vehicle, while Nissan's reputation was linked more to the quality of its engineering. The way of the competitive market, though, is reflected in what happens in the intervening two decades. In the next 20 years Jeep has improved its quality, Nissan has improved its ruggedness and the two brands have become similar on several other dimensions.

Moon's work identifies a natural dynamic in the marketplace. Good people, working hard to improve their products and services by offsetting deficiencies, have a natural tendency to become more like their rivals. But in spite of this natural tendency toward sameness, why do some firms still rise above the pack? In his widely cited work on competitive rationality,[2] Peter Dickson suggests that there are three innate drivers of entrepreneurial behavior in a competitive marketplace: the drive to improve customer satisfaction, to reduce process costs, and to improve process efficiency. The energy that fuels these drivers is the *desire to learn*. People and organizations who can learn the most quickly about variation in demand and supply will tend to be the most competitive. Leveraging these drives along with the natural differences that exist among customers (demand heterogeneity), some firms essentially experiment by introducing new product or service variations. The "improve my deficiency" tendency that Moon identifies is nested in the innovation-imitation process, that is, successful experiments are copied by competitors. At the same time, though, customers in such markets become more sensitive to, and come to seek, new variations that *better* meet demand. Drawing on classic work in economics, Dickson builds into his model the notion that luck favors prepared and alert firms, for example, *innovators* who have a deep understanding of how customer expectations are changing and *imitators* who watch and think about market reactions before blindly mimicking competitors' actions. The most competitive firms are those that have the strongest drive to learn and improve.

Market dynamics are about a constant search for differentiation that can, paradoxically, lead to "sameness." Yet Dickson's work reminds us that there are firms who continuously lead the way out of commoditization by having greater perceptual acuity—by understanding their markets in a manner superior to the competition. Here in chapter 8, we consider both how the 3-Circle model describes and reveals market dynamics, and then how the model can help in anticipating likely actions of customers and how competitors can improve growth strategy. The market does not stand still—it is dynamic. To that end, this chapter explains how value moves through the 3-Circle model by demonstrating how markets and competitors change and how competitive advantage shifts over time. Building upon the research of D'Aveni, Mintzberg, Miller and Friesen, and others we demonstrate how customer values and needs, competitors market positioning, and a company's own resource bundling may change the market landscape.[3] We begin with an important and dramatic illustration of market dynamics.

Johnson & Johnson Stent:
The Perfect Market-Dynamics Storm[4]

Johnson & Johnson (J&J) developed the first working "stent," a small medical implement that could be used for patients with artery blockages in lieu of open heart surgery. A tiny metal "scaffold" that is inserted into an artery during a balloon angioplasty procedure, the stent significantly cuts down the rates of the artery collapsing after angioplasty and, as a result, reduces the probability of follow-up emergency surgery.

Over 7 years in the late 1980s and early 1990s, J&J invested in the research and development of the stent and compiled the research necessary to gain regulatory approval. The product was an immediate success, quickly building a $1-billion market, even though the stent was too new to be covered by health insurance. Having pioneered the development effort, J&J held a well-deserved 90% of that market in 1996. This product alone accounted for a significant proportion of the consumer-products giant's operating income. Cleveland Clinic physician Eric Topal described the J&J Palmaz-Schatz stent as "changing cardiology and the treatment of coronary-artery disease forever." Despite all this success, by the end of 1998, J&J *lost all but 8% of its market share.*

J&J faced several challenges after introducing the stent to the market. First, the J&J Palmaz-Schatz stent was initially so successful that demand substantially exceeded supply. As a result, one of the company's initial challenges was making enough stents to meet demand. On top of that, two other initiatives were consuming significant company attention and resources. To facilitate its move into medical devices, J&J had acquired angioplasty balloon-maker Cordis, a merger made particularly challenging by Cordis's entrepreneurial culture that conflicted with J&J's top-down culture. In addition, J&J was allocating significant resources to lobbying the insurance industry to obtain insurance coverage for the stent. At introduction, the company had priced the stent at $1,595, a significant new expense for hospitals that was not covered by existing reimbursement levels for angioplasty procedures.

Customer Response

While doctors (and, by extension, their patients) were happy with the stent's initial performance, hospital administrators had difficulty with its cost. Despite pressure from hospitals for price breaks, J&J stood by its price of $1,595. The company would not give quantity discounts, requiring many hospitals to carry new, significant budget expenses for the stent. Many hospitals felt gouged by J&J, perceived to be a consumer-products firm (the "baby shampoo" company) and a newcomer to the medical implements market. They felt that J&J was holding hospitals hostage by flexing its pricing power.

Market Learning

As J&J focused on building capacity, lobbying the insurance industry, and integrating a new firm with a very different culture, the company was unable to respond to feedback from doctors for improving on the first-generation stent. The original J&J stent came in only one size (about 5/8 of an inch) and was made of relatively inflexible, bare metal. The doctors learned quickly and expressed a very clear need for stents of different sizes and flexibilities to improve ease of use.

Competitor Response

J&J had built an honest advantage in pioneering the stent market, but the company also paid the price often paid by a first-mover innovator. The company carried the product through research, development, and regulatory approval, creating both a knowledge base and market opportunity for other fast followers. Paying close attention to market reaction to the one-size, bare-metal J&J stent, competitor Guidant's subsequent success in this market was built upon J&J's early research and market development investments and learning: (a) Guidant was able to develop the more flexible stents that physicians were demanding, (b) Guidant and other rivals benefited from both J&J's groundwork and physicians' pushing the FDA to speed up the approval process for new stents, and (c) J&J was successful in achieving a $2,600 increase in insurance coverage for angioplasty procedures to cover the cost of a stent exactly one day before Guidant introduced its new stent product on the U.S. market.

Understanding Market Needs

J&J's subsequent dramatic loss of market share resulted from a significant store of resentment that had built up through its holding the line on its $1,595 price point and its inability to adequately address physician concerns about flexibility and ease of use. J&J's behavior was driven by a solid belief in its pricing (which was later validated by rivals' entry pricing) and the allocation of resources to other tasks. Doctors and hospitals interpreted the company's apparent lack of responsiveness to a failure to understand the needs of this new market. While J&J was in some ways a victim of awful luck, ultimately, the customer's perception of how a firm responds to its circumstances is the real determinant of its market share.

The J&J story is told neither to lament the company's situation in the stent market (they have since continued to innovate and to effectively compete in this market) nor to focus on a great idea gone awry. It is instead told to illustrate an extreme example of the innovation-imitation cycles that Dickson describes in his model of competitive rationality, as well as the fact that the fastest learner in a market often gets an advantage. In addition, it allows us to consider how the 3-Circle model captures such dynamics.

Market Dynamics in 3 Circles

In previous chapters, there has been a strong theme of value dynamics. Beginning in chapter 2, we showed how movement of the circles could illustrate commoditization. Integral to chapter 4 was a discussion of key lessons about attributes and benefits that can evolve from differentiators to parity to nonvalue, while chapter 6 presented a way to think about growth strategy as value shifting between different areas of the model. Here, we review the two general types of dynamics that provide some diagnostic value for anticipating future behavior in the market.

Dynamic Type 1: Value Flows Through the Circles

A key point throughout the earlier chapters is that one can think of attributes and benefits as having different roles over time. While this is not a new idea it is embedded in the work of Kano (1995) and Gale (1994), it is an idea that is not really captured in a life-cycle flow in other models. Figure 8.1 (part A) shows what we might expect to be a typical flow of value in a market. New ideas or innovations, like the stent, emerge by providing new technology or methods for better resolving unmet needs. Once developed and commercialized, such innovative attributes become a firm's Area A. So J&J initially had a near monopoly on stent sales with a distinctive Area A. Yet competitive imitation pushes once-distinctive attributes and benefits into Area B, where they become, at best, points of parity. In fact, continuing the path, one can see that for many patients, doctors would prefer new, flexible stents, suggesting that the bare-metal stent (although still on the market) may, for many situations, fall into Area D or even out of the model, that is, not even in the consideration set for certain procedures.

If we think of an attribute life cycle, we might consider that attributes or benefits similarly pass through different phases of introduction, growth,

There are two ways that the 3 circles can represent the dynamic nature of markets

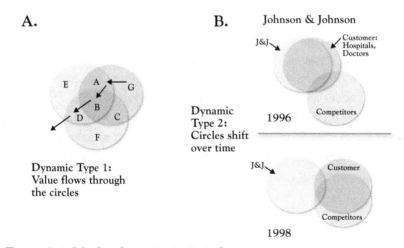

Figure 8.1. Market dynamics in 3 circles.

maturity, and decline, as reflected in the classic product life cycle theory. As noted, the original one-size, inflexible, bare-metal stents quickly lost favor and gave way to more flexible stents. But the market kept moving quickly from there. When it was discovered that there could be a build-up of scar tissue around an implanted stent over time, J&J once again innovated in creating a drug-eluting stent that provided for the timed-release of blood-thinning drugs to prevent clotting. However, Boston Scientific has fought J&J for this business, with market share going back and forth, along with lawsuits over patent challenges. Different types of drugs (e.g., transplant drugs vs. cancer drugs) have been used for drug-eluting stents, further increasing the variation in offerings. Stent manufacturers and vascular specialists have discovered other stent applications as the category has evolved. Fighting 700,000 strokes a year, stents for the carotid artery have been developed, credited with significant improvement in stroke prevention and reducing the need for surgery. Nonvascular stents have been developed for clearing blockages in kidneys, intestines, and lungs. Each of these value-added variations occupies a different place in the 3-Circle model for a given manufacturer, depending on the relative uniqueness of its offering relative to competitors.

Dynamic Type 2: Circles Shift Over Time

One of the most useful and powerful ways the 3-Circle graphics can convey the implications of thoughtful customer and competitor research (and subsequent action) is in the conceptual meaning behind the movement of the circles. There are three basic types of movements:

- *One of the firms moves closer to the customer circle.* A competitor who has improved its value delivery on dimensions important to the customer will find an increase in overlap between its circle and the customer's circle. This can be identified conceptually and is based on measurement of customer value, as the firm's scores on dimensions more important to customers improve. The service firm who improves its speed of service delivery, the educational institution that more effectively connects its students to opportunities, the technology product that improves the user's efficiency to get a greater sense of

control—all move the firm's circle closer, creating greater overlap with fundamental customer needs. Depending on various
product failures or recalls in the stent market, J&J and Boston
Scientific continue to go back and forth in terms of market
share. In 3-Circle terms this is like a moving picture over time
in which the two firms alternate in their degree of overlap with
the customer circle.

- *The circles for both competitors move closer to the customer's circle.*
  When innovation-imitation cycles kick in, the net effect is that
  both competitors converge on the customer's circle. From a
  societal allocation of resources perspective, this is a positive—
  the customer gets more value. From a competitive strategy
  perspective, it may be less desired if the follower is simply
  matching the value added by the innovator, creating a commodity market.

- *The customer's circle shifts away from both competitors' circles.* As
  substitute technologies emerge, it is frequently the case that
  customers find value in new sources. This may be a transition
  that happens very quickly (e.g., the MP3 player over portable
  CD players) or it may be slower. In either case, the firm's ability to pick up on changes in customer purchasing behavior and
  attitudes is critical.

Referring back to Figure 8.1, part B demonstrates the shift in circles
capturing J&J's decline in the stent market in 1996 through 1998. Our
post-hoc interpretation of this unusual situation is straightforward. The
combination of new competitive offerings that effectively met customers'
developing needs *and* built up resentment toward J&J for perceived price
gouging and nonresponse on new product development led to a situation
in which the competitor's circle essentially took over the customer's circle
while pushing J&J nearly out of the picture.

Anticipating Market Dynamics

In earlier chapters, we have discussed analysis of customer value in a way
that prompts growth strategy development. Ultimately, though, the growth
strategies you propose need to be vetted. Our vetting process here first

requires you to look closely at whether you have, or could get, the resources needed to effectively execute the growth strategy (chapter 7). Next, though, is to think through how your growth strategies will fit as market conditions change and how those strategies may change the market.

The term *dynamics* is about change—how is the market likely to change in the future in part as a function of implementing a new growth strategy? Thinking "dynamically" is difficult. It means evaluating a decision as a game theorist might: anticipating decision options the firm might have, thinking about how different players in the market (customers, competitors) will react over time to each decision option by stepping into the shoes of those players, then working back from these anticipated outcomes to select the best option. It turns out that such predictions are often so uncertain and complex, that we just avoid the issue![5] Such dynamics can only be estimated with great uncertainty.

Our goal in concluding the chapter is to provoke some thinking about how to get your hands around the likely dynamics that your new growth strategies will face. It is beyond the scope of this chapter to provide a detailed analysis of market dynamics to cover all types of growth strategies, but we will plant a few seeds here for analysis and subsequent study. We will address anticipation of the dynamic aspects of customer, competitors, and capabilities.

Anticipating Customer Dynamics

A variety of theories—from the product life cycle to competitive rationality—help us understand that customer preferences will change over time. There are two primary reasons for this. First, there may be a natural change in customer preferences and demand to external environmental events. The rapid increase in fuel costs in the past few years has significantly affected customer value and associated attributes that they began to demand from the producers of automobiles. Toyota introduced the first widely accepted hybrid technology in the Prius and enjoyed a significant Area A around the hybrid technology. Since then, a number of other auto manufacturers have developed hybrid versions of their vehicles. A second driver of changes in customer preferences is the rate of innovation-imitation cycles themselves. Dickson (1997) noted in his book *Marketing Management* that between 1987 and 1992, the mountain bike market share grew from 12% to 58% of the overall bicycle market. This remarkable jump was not due to consumers waking up one morning with visions that they must have a mountain bike. Instead, it resulted from the experimentation of one bike manufacturer that was quickly imitated by others, creating a spike in the amount and variation of *supply*, which unearthed significant customer demand.

While there is no precise science of customer value dynamics we can summarize some important principles as follows:

- *Over time, as products become more alike, customers will become more price driven and tougher negotiators.* This is the first thing business people tend to think about as markets mature. In the pioneering work that introduced the concept of cocreation in the business press, C. K. Prahalad and Venkat Ramaswamy describe today's marketplace as one in which customers are increasingly powerful:

  > It's perfectly feasible for a customer to approach a bank and say, "I will always leave a $5,000 balance in the bank. These are the services I want free in return for this commitment." . . . A customer at one telecom provider, a heavy user of long-distance services, even obtained preferential long-distance rates in exchange for a commitment to that provider.[6]

- *This tendency is a natural outcome of more and better information for customers today, particularly via the Internet.* Yet it is more significantly a function of the similarity in products that emerge as markets mature. As we have emphasized throughout this book, striving to deeply understand the value customers seek and producing unique solutions is an important strategic priority. As markets evolve, though, it is equally important to understand how to give customers an additional hand in this process.
- *Over time, customers will learn how features of a product or service link to their consumption problems and benefits desired.* We once conducted an exploratory study of consumers who had recently purchased computers for their homes. We preselected

half of those interviewed to be novices (first-time purchasers) and half to be experts (very experienced with purchasing and using computers). The difference between them was straightforward. The experts spoke in terms of how different types of computer features could be used for particular applications and what attribute levels were needed to accomplish particular goals. In short, they understood how to translate benefits into the task that needed to be done. In contrast, the novices' basic approach was to take a newspaper ad for a computer to a retail salesperson or to an expert at work and to ask, "Are these the features I need?" In sum, the novices needed a translator! Essentially, experience leads to an ability to speak two languages: the language of features and the language of desired outcomes and results, and to be able to translate one to another.

- *Over time, as customers learn, they will add value if you let them.* A still-developing, yet very important paradigm in the business press today is "cocreation." In purest form, cocreation refers to a scenario in which firm and customer together define the product or service experience. An extreme form of cocreation is when users "take over" a brand, as Alex Wipperfurth describes in his book *Brand Hijack.*[7] There is a more basic research tradition around *lead users* that was pioneered by Eric von Hippel of MIT, which explores how to leverage the ideas of innovative customers in product and service development.[8] Von Hippel's work has been seminal in helping firms understanding the role of customers in leading innovation. Cocreation, though, formalizes discussion of a new layer of value that emerges from the customer's *ownership* in the ideas that emerge. An interesting example is the secret menu that customers codeveloped at In-N-Out Burger, a restaurant with a cult following and a very simple 4-item menu: burgers, fries, shakes, and soft drinks. The secret menu developed in response to customers' special requests for variations of the menu (e.g., the "wish burger" is a vegetarian option not on the menu and named by customers). There is significant potential here for Area-G thinking as the product or service matures, and it exists in the thinking of the very people using the product.

The key question as you develop strategy should be, is your growth idea subject to these dynamics in a way that will reduce its probability of success? Or, can you leverage these forces to enhance your Area A?

Anticipating Competitor Dynamics

Customer learning and evolving participation can certainly have a significant impact on growth strategy as it develops. However, it is also important to note that the reactions of competitors can have an enormous impact on the success or failure of a new growth strategy. Northwest Airlines, for example, cut its prices on a route critical to a smaller regional competitor when that competitor slashed its prices on one of Northwest's key routes, completely neutralizing the smaller rival's strategy. But as we have noted, there is a fair amount of evidence suggesting that managers may not often take the time to anticipate competitor reactions. Interestingly, this may not be harmful, as there may be many circumstances in which competitors actually may not respond to particular moves. However, the likelihood of a competitive response to your new growth strategy will be a function of the degree of threat as perceived by the competitor. In a recent *Harvard Business Review* article, McKinsey consultants Kevin Coyne and John Horn provide a very practical template for thinking through the odds that competitors will react to your actions, organized around the following questions:[9]

- *Will your rival see your actions?* Coyne and Horn's empirical research suggests that firms often do not observe rivals' actions until it is too late to respond.
- *Will the competitor feel threatened?* Here, it is important to get a sense of the rival's goals for the product or service lines that might be affected.
- *Will mounting a response be a priority for the competitor?* Of everything on the competitor's plate, will reacting to your new strategy be a priority?
- *Can your rival overcome organizational inertia?* Coyne and Horn point out the very real organizational barrier that reactions will require resource allocations and external commitments that the rival may find too cumbersome to overcome.

The first four questions all speak to gauging the probability that a competitor will even respond to your new growth strategy. This leads to another set of questions under the assumption that a reaction will be forthcoming:

- *If the competitor is likely to respond,*
  - o what options will the competitor actively consider;
  - o which option will the competitor most likely choose?

The authors' research suggests that competitors are likely to consider two to three options. Further, they suggest that much insight can be gained into predicting the competitor's likely reaction if our team can put themselves in the rivals shoes by thinking through (a) the number of moves the rival is likely to look ahead and (b) the particular metrics the competitor is likely to use.

In all, Coyne and Horn's framework provides an excellent series of prompts for considering whether competitor reactions to your new growth strategy are forthcoming and what actions are likely to be considered. But if the competitor is probably going to react to our new growth strategy, the question is, what is our next move? Here, we need to return to capabilities, which are themselves dynamic.

Capability Dynamics

Despite decades of industry leadership and a large Area A, in the early 1990s, IBM's stock price plummeted, 60,000 employees were dismissed, and Wall Street had written the company off.[10] Like a driver stuck in the sand, IBM executives thought that if they spun their tires just a little bit longer, using the same tried and true strategies and resources, they could regain market leadership and move forward again. Louis Gerstner, who became IBM CEO in 1993, said that the company lost its market in the early 1990s because "all of [IBM's] capabilities were of a business model that had fallen wildly out of step with marketplace realities."[11] In chapter 7, we described how successful companies become entrenched with the resources, capabilities, and assets that made them successful and become out of touch with changing customer values. This view was supported by Chandler's research, where he found that successful companies typically pursue the same strategies and competencies that brought them success, and yet, they are fatal in the long run.[12]

Harreld et al. described how IBM's leadership used dynamic capabilities to redefine itself and regain and sustain market leadership. Dynamic capabilities require company executives to first "sense" or anticipate opportunities in the market. For IBM, this meant sensing new market opportunities through exploration and learning. Gerstner, IBM's new CEO, forecasted that, over the next decade, "customers would increasingly value companies that could provide solutions-solutions that integrated technology from various suppliers and, more importantly integrated technology into the processes of the enterprise."[13]

While anticipating new customer value propositions is necessary to firm positioning, execution is the key to delivering the value and capturing the market. An organization with dynamic capability is able to quickly and effectively adjust and restructure its internal resources, capabilities, and assets to capture the anticipated opportunities. Gerstner's internal analysis of the firm's capabilities found that IBM had intelligent and talented employees and that its problems were not with its technology. The primary problem was that IBM failed to build and configure bundles of resources, capabilities, and assets necessary to meet the needs of the changing market. IBM leveraged and reconfigured its resources and, in the process, provided the type of value desired by customers— value that was rare in the market and could not be easily imitated by the competition. Among other things, they created internal computer software technology with "open architecture, integrated processes and self-managing systems" to help IBM employees communicate better within the company and to quickly respond to customer needs. The change in the way information is managed within IBM has modified the internal capabilities and assets of the company, transforming the market brand from a computer-hardware to a computer-services business.[14] In short, IBM created a strong Area A, a competitive advantage.

Companies that anticipate or "sense" changes in customer value and have dynamic rather than static internal capabilities gain and sustain Area A advantages. In short, the 3-Circle model shifts as organizations anticipate external customer value by dynamically altering their internal competencies.

Chapter Summary

The effective development of growth strategy not only needs to account for the current and future state of customer value and competitive behavior, it also needs to consider how those states of nature will change. Here, we have reviewed some basic tendencies in competitive markets that tend to evolve toward commoditization until a perceptive, fast-learning firm can move it in a different direction. We have also seen how such dynamics can be captured in the 3-Circle framework. Dynamics bring to mind that life and marketplace competitions have some circular elements to them—patterns repeat, influence one another, and the folks who get the quickest understanding of the value sought in the system often end up winning. It is not an endless cycle, however. We have defined a series of 10 discrete steps that will help form the basis for a productive growth strategy project. Our next chapter brings the discussion of growth strategy full circle by summarizing the overall process for strategy development that integrates the core concepts of the first eight chapters.

CHAPTER 9

Summary

Growth Strategy in 10 Steps

This book is based on a fairly simple premise, one that is not new: the firm that develops a better understanding of the value that customers seek has a competitive advantage. What is new, however, is the realistic look at just how difficult it is to develop that understanding. It is a long shot from simply "giving customers what they want." It instead means developing an understanding of the deep drivers of customer value sought, shoring up our value proposition in the short term, but then building a longer-term, unique position that speaks to those customer values. We find, over and over again, that there are gaps between what managers currently believe customers value and believe and actual customer assessments. There is growth opportunity in closing these gaps, and the 3-Circle strategy process is precisely designed to uncover and leverage that opportunity.

In this chapter, we summarize the work by presenting the 10-step process in which a growth strategy project is defined and executed (see figure 9.1). There are really three big elements underlying these 10 steps. First is for the management team to formally lay out the scope of the project and then their hypotheses about customer value (Steps 1 and 2a). Second is to gather data directly from target customers and to analyze it by breaking it down into the categories defined in the model and deeper analysis via laddering (Steps 2b, 3, and 4). Third is to develop particular growth strategy ideas and test them out via (a) assessment of capabilities required and alignment, and (b) evaluating the competitive dynamics of the marketplace. By Step 10, we have developed a growth strategy that has been developed upon the sound foundation of customer value analysis and screened by a deep analysis of capabilities, resources, and assets.

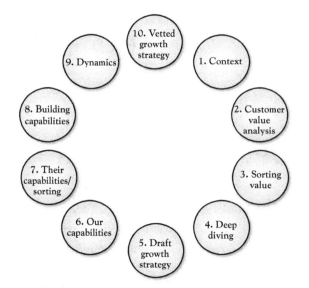

Figure 9.1. Ten steps in a 3-Circle growth strategy project.

To illustrate this process, we will use the case study of a major global pharmaceuticals firm.

Step 1: Defining Context

In fact, chapter 4 has covered Step 1 in fair detail. It is essential that we have a clear sense of the parameters of the project, in the form of the now familiar context statement:

> "My goal is to grow **COMPANY UNIT** by creating more value for **CUSTOMER SEGMENT** than **COMPETITOR** does."

Annie Lambert is a brand manager at MedFactor,[1] an $8-billion worldwide manufacturer of pharmaceuticals, who led a 3-Circle project for her company. The goal for the context statement was "to grow sales and profit of MedFactor's OptiMod drug by creating more value for specialist doctors than PharmaRival does with its drug Vivatrol."

Step 2: Customer Analysis

Recall from chapter 4 ("The Meaning of Value") that the underlying factor behind a successful competitive strategy is superior understanding of what drives *the value being sought by customers*. We can wander back through the chapters and see this in many examples: DuPont's success with Teflon came only after its management team understood the important values behind consumers value placed on time savings (as opposed to healthy eating); Ultimate Ears' phenomenal success was due to the enormous value placed by musicians on superior performance and safety, values less known before in-ear monitors were invented simply because on-stage monitors were taken as a "given"; Accor was successful with the spartan Formule 1 hotel design because they understood that a large segment of customers simply sought rest and safety in a clean, quiet place to sleep; providing for this specific experience at a bargain price made Formule 1 very successful.

Yet we need a systematic way to think about value. Step 2 involves uncovering the dimensions of value—first to understand executives' best guesses as to customer value (Step 2a) and then to obtain customers' actual perceived value (Step 2b). Recall from chapter 4 that value can be broken down in a simple way:

$$\text{Value}_j = \sum_{i=1}^{n} *I_i.$$

This equation simply implies that a customer's assessment of the overall value of brand j can be broken down to be a function of what the customer believes about brand j on each of up to n attributes, each weighted by their importance. There is a long line of research in psychology and marketing that uses this formulation to determine overall brand assessments by taking individual consumer beliefs about the brand—for example, B_{ij}—the consumer's belief about brand j on attribute i—each weighted by I_i, the importance of attribute i to the consumer. This, again, is a straightforward way to think about overall value—there are some critical pieces of information that come out of this model that help us dig more deeply into customer value:

- There are attributes or benefits on which customers base their evaluations.

- These attributes/benefits vary in their importance.
- Customers have varying beliefs about the competitive brands on these attributes.

It turns out that this is enough information to make some significant strides in understanding customer value and growth opportunities.

In the case of our pharmaceuticals example, assume that Annie and her executive team initially identified the following six key attributes and benefits as key reasons why doctors in this category would choose one brand over another (again, this was *before* speaking to the doctors):

- Dosing options (variety of strength levels)
- Drug efficacy
- Familiarity with or trust in brand
- Adequacy of managed care coverage
- Drug tolerability
- Drug half-life

The executive team made their estimates of customer value before any doctors were interviewed. This exercise required the executives to estimate both how important they believe the previous attributes are to the doctors and how the doctors are likely to rate both their brand Opti-Mod and the competitive brand Vivatrol on each attribute. Subsequently, Annie interviewed a sample of specialist doctors, asking them to provide ratings in a format similar to those provided by the MedFactor team. In addition, open-ended questions were asked about other attributes or benefits the doctors believe influence their prescription decisions and the important values behind the key reasons. These questions proved insightful, as they revealed two other attributes that were important to doctors in evaluating competitive drugs: the *availability of clinical evidence* and *sales-force experience*.

Step 3: Sorting Value

Step 3 involves the actual sorting of value into the seven categories defined by the 3-Circle model. As we have emphasized throughout the book, each of these categories has implications for growth strategies. Together, they summarize most of the core concepts of current work on growth strategy. For MedFactor's drug OptiMod, Annie's analysis based on interviews with several specialist physicians revealed a number of important insights (see Figure 9.2 for a summary). The analysis illustrates a classic case of a new brand facing an entrenched existing brand with whom physicians are quite familiar. Annie's drug OptiMod gets unique credit from physicians only for its flexibility in dosage levels (Area A). In contrast, the competitor's Vivatrol is a very familiar drug with which physicians have a great deal of experience. It is also perceived by physicians to have an advantage on the managed-care side, meaning that they believe the patient will pay less and be better served by insurance coverage for Vivatrol compared to OptiMod.

Surprise Insights

The Figure 9.2 analysis captures physician perceptions as Annie identified them in the interviews. However, two critical points came as a complete surprise:

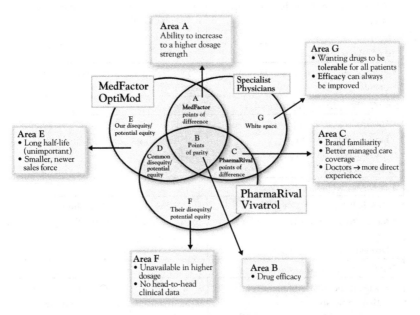

Figure 9.2. Three-circle analysis for MedFactor's new drug.

- **Area B**: While the two brands were perceived by doctors to be equivalent in efficacy, a head-to-head trial showed statistically significant improvement symptom relief for Annie's brand OptiMod over Vivatrol.
- **Area C**: Vivatrol was perceived by the doctors to have an advantage in managed-care coverage in spite of the fact there is objectively no difference between OptiMod and Vivatrol on this dimension.

These two insights were quite significant but there was more. In addition to the earlier findings of important customer attributes that the executive team had not included in their original list, the physicians volunteered that two other factors were influential in their assessments of the two companies and their drugs: laboratory evidence and sales-force experience.

Table 9.1. 3-Circle Model Areas and Generic Growth Questions

Current model area/analysis	Generic growth question
Area A: Our points of difference	
• Ability to increase to a higher dosage strength	How do we identify, build, and defend differentiation that is meaningful to customers?
Area B: Points of parity	
• Efficacy perceived to be similar across brands	How do we maintain points of parity to remain "at parity?"
Area C: Their points of difference	
• Vivatrol is more familiar, doctors have more experience with it • Vivatrol is perceived to offer better managed care coverage	Should we neutralize competitors' differentiation? (If so, how?) Or should we live and let live?
Area E: Disequity or potential equity	
• Drug half-life • MedFactor has a relatively small sales force • No evidence of efficacy	How do we correct, reduce/eliminate disequities, OR reveal equities that customers are unaware of?
Area G: White space (unmet needs)	
• There are individual differences in patients' tolerance of and response to these drugs	How can we identify totally new growth ideas around customers' unmet needs?

Step 4: Deep Diving

Throughout the book, we have alluded to the importance of understanding customer value from a deeper perspective. In sum, behind the customer attributes we have identified are the deeper reasons or values we discussed in chapter 4. In Annie's case, she wanted to focus on what she found to be the most important attribute to doctors—efficacy. Efficacy is shorthand for effectiveness—to what extent does the drug produce the desired remedy? Figure 9.3 presents the ladder that summarizes Annie's conversations with doctors regarding the reasons why efficacy is an important driver of decisions. This insight is straightforward: doctors do not seek to prescribe a particular drug simply because it is more efficacious—the efficacy is important because it reinforces the doctor's sense of fulfillment in helping improve patients' quality of life. While in hindsight this seems obvious, in fact it is not obvious at all if you do not ask the questions. The product's positioning and communications can be much more powerful if it is connected to the customer's deeper values (i.e., there will be a greater sense of patient care and personal satisfaction for this objectively better drug). Further, understanding the doctor's goal at a deeper level gets us thinking about how to both communicate and, in thinking through broader solutions, support his or her efforts—for example, by developing new ways to ensure that patients take required dosages.

The deeper values behind drug efficacy

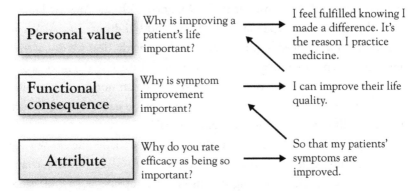

Figure 9.3. Ladder for doctors on the attribute efficacy.

Step 5: Preliminary Growth Strategy Ideas

The categories of value identified in Step 3 (sorting) and additional insights from the research generate some natural, action-oriented questions for pursuing growth of customer value and competitive position. In chapter 6, we discussed a series of growth questions that naturally emerge from the different categories of the framework. For Annie's case, the questions led to a number of preliminary growth ideas, which are presented in the text boxes surrounding the 3-Circle diagram in Figure 9.4. The figure exhibits the value that Annie discovered in her interviews in Column A and the basic growth questions for each category of value in Column B. Column C indicates the conclusions initially drawn by this analysis. Chief among these conclusions was to correct doctor's misperceptions regarding OptiMod's efficacy and managed-care coverage. We will come to the final conclusions regarding growth strategy in Step 10.

Steps 6, 7, and 8: Exploring Capabilities, Resources, and Assets to Align Behind Growth Strategy Ideas

Refer back to Figure 9.1 for a moment. Once growth ideas are initially generated in Step 5, then the important questions revolve around (a) whether or not we can substantively deliver upon those unique ideas, or (b) whether we might want to cut costs by reducing those capabilities or assets that are not contributing effectively to customer value. So Step 6 begins the process of grounding growth strategy in our existing and potential future capabilities. The questions here are what capabilities do we actually have? Are those capabilities aligned with our Area A? Do we have the substantive capabilities to defend and build our Area A? What capabilities do we need to pursue each of the growth ideas we discovered in Step 5? Step 7 then takes the necessary step of turning the microscope to competitors' organizations in order to provide an honest look at ourselves. Do we really have capabilities, resources, or assets that are in any way truly different from those of competitors?

Figure 9.5 provides a partial analysis of what we label the *inside view* for Annie and her firm MedFactor versus PharmaRival. As noted in chapter 8, the two circles reflecting the inside view capture skills and assets *inside* the firm. The easiest way to identify the relationship between the

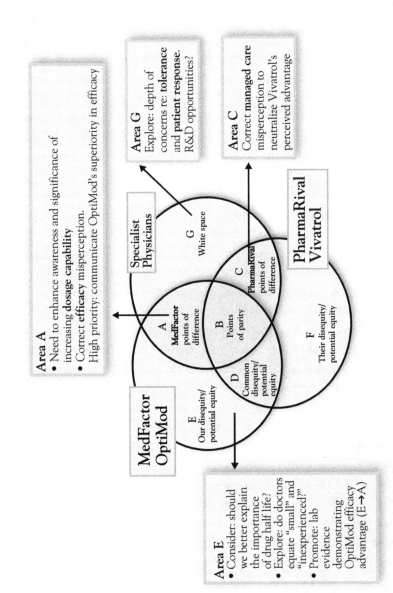

Area A
- Need to enhance awareness and significance of increasing **dosage capability**
- Correct **efficacy** misperception.

High priority: communicate OptiMod's superiority in efficacy

Area G
Explore: depth of concerns re: **tolerance** and **patient response**. R&D opportunities?

Area C
Correct **managed care** misperception to neutralize Vivatrol's perceived advantage

Specialist Physicians

PharmaRival Vivatrol

MedFactor OptiMod

G
White space

A
MedFactor points of difference

C
PharmaRival points of difference

B
Points of parity

D
Common disequity/ potential equity

E
Our disequity/ potential equity

F
Their disequity/ potential equity

Area E
- Consider: should we better explain the importance of drug half life?
- Explore: do doctors equate "small" and "inexperienced?"
- Promote: lab evidence demonstrating OptiMod efficacy advantage (E→A)

Figure 9.4. Growth strategy priorities for OptiMod.

inside view (two circles capturing capabilities) and the outside view (three circles capturing customers' perception of needs and the ability of each player to meet those needs) is to think of cause and effect. The inside view *causes* the outside view. In other words, the customer benefits that we find in the customer's assessment (the outside view) are actually *produced by* the capabilities, resources, and assets that we enumerate in the inside view. So the firm maximizes its competitive advantage and financial outcomes when it develops skills and resources that both (a) generate unique benefits for customers and (b) cannot be easily matched by competitors. The problem with the standard literature on the resource-based view of the firm is that it provides no mechanism by which resources and capabilities are connected to unique customer value.[2] In the analysis here, the mechanism is a careful set of questions that ask the analyst to evaluate both the existing points of difference and the potential growth ideas against the capabilities that should be in place to make them happen. Annie's analysis for MedFactor in Figure 9.5 suggests that the firm appears to have a unique capability *advantage* in product development and potentially a unique capability *disadvantage* in the sales force (both size and organization or discipline). The analysis suggests that MedFactor's Area A with OptiMod (higher dosage potential) is unique to the product and, along with an actual advantage in efficacy, is likely attributable to a better new product development capability. The jury is still out on whether or not these product advantages are sustainable. In this case, however, it was clear that some growth issues could be addressed specifically through more effective communications and building the sales force's skills and tool kit around the specific hot-button issues in the value proposition—specifically, OptiMod's currently underappreciated efficacy advantage and the misperception about the managed-care disadvantage.

Step 9 involves an analysis of market dynamics depicted in the three circles. This step recognizes that markets are constantly moving, and in potentially predictable ways. Recall from chapter 8 that changes in the market can be reflected one of two ways in the model. First, the circles move, often approaching one another as the offerings of the different competitors become more similar and customer needs become more well known as a product or service category matures. Second, though, is the flow of value through the circles, which helps illustrate the typical competitive innovation-imitation cycle of healthy markets.

MedFactor vs. PharmaRival
The Inside View

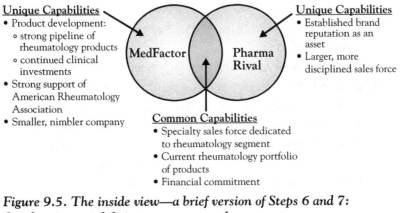

Unique Capabilities
- Product development:
  - strong pipeline of rheumatology products
  - continued clinical investments
- Strong support of American Rheumatology Association
- Smaller, nimbler company

MedFactor

Pharma Rival

Unique Capabilities
- Established brand reputation as an asset
- Larger, more disciplined sales force

Common Capabilities
- Specialty sales force dedicated to rheumatology segment
- Current rheumatology portfolio of products
- Financial commitment

Figure 9.5. The inside view—a brief version of Steps 6 and 7: Overlapping capabilities, resources, and assets.

In the case of MedFactor and its drug OptiMod, the market dynamics analysis would suggest that once the firm is able to establish its unique Area A with doctors, there is a very real possibility that its advantages can be eroded over time as its competitors seek to imitate its unique advantages. A careful exploration of the forces that evolve the market toward commoditization is imperative, as patent protection is limited and other firms are likely to be aggressive in their imitation of a demonstrated competitive advantage.

Step 10: Vetted Growth Strategy

Ultimately, the ideas behind growth strategy evolve and improve through the iterative evaluation in Steps 6 through 9 of the 10-step process. The first screen is customer value. The second screen includes capabilities, resources, and assets. The third screen addresses market dynamics. In the end, the goal is to develop growth strategy that will hit the most important customer values in the most efficient way. The OptiMod team developed and executed their growth strategy for the brand in three specific ways. The following is paraphrased from Annie's report:

Reposition "EFFICACY" from Area B to Area A. A notable theme throughout this analysis is that there are key benefits to be leveraged for OptiMod of which the customer is not fully aware. From the outside view, efficacy is a point of parity between the two products (Area B) but it actually is an attribute that could be leveraged for OptiMod (Area A) because of the favorable head-to-head study results.

Optimize Area A. Dosing is an important attribute to specialist doctors in this category and is a point of difference for OptiMod. Communicate the dosing feature as a point of difference between Vivatrol and OptiMod when a rheumatologist views efficacy as being the same. Create shelf talkers to communicate the key dosing messages for OptiMod at the point of selection. Enhance prominence of dosing message on sales material.

Moving from Area C to B. Doctors are under the misconception that Vivatrol has managed care advantages over OptiMod. Sales force should educate doctors on managed care position of OptiMod in local areas. Create geography-specific shelf talkers that highlight formulary coverage of OptiMod vs. competition.

In addition, doctors are more familiar with PharmaRival than MedFactor. Develop awareness campaign & corporate branding initiatives that highlight MedFactor's current commitment to rheumatology and future pipeline. Ensure key opinion leaders in the field are aware of points of difference about MedFactor as opposed to product differentiation only. Continue to partner with professional associations to improve the awareness of the MedFactor name.[3]

MedFactor put five different corporate branding initiatives into place in order to improve awareness of the company name with customers. In addition, the company has also addressed the problem of its managed care positioning. MedFactor put two new sales tools in place that feature local formulary grids. This enabled its sales representatives to review the information with customers—and show them how it is relevant to their local business.

The actions undertaken by the MedFactor team were very successful. The new branding initiatives contributed to a 20% growth in prescription volume for OptiMod in fiscal year 2009. Fueled by truly superior product value and communications that effectively demonstrated that value, the brand took over the market leadership position in its category during that year. The key competitive strategy concerns that Annie and her team identified on the basis of interviewing physicians in the key target market tended to focus on *education*. They found fairly clear consistency around the need for evidence in demonstrating one's advantages and the company's failure to effectively share that evidence. In general, there is lower risk in making big decisions regarding education even on the basis of small sample evidence as, very frequently, more education is better, provided that (a) it is focused on the right customer values, and (b) the company really, truly effectively delivers on those customer values.

Chapter Summary

Beating the competitor, creating value for customers, and building capabilities may be seen as goals or principles that are often at odds with one another. So most firms tend to focus on one or two of those goals. The search for growth is further complicated by the fact that knowledge of customer needs can get quickly out of date even though we feel confident in our existing knowledge. The imperative here is first to narrow the focus to the three core principles, to focus on understanding customer value as primary, but then to also think of those principles as an integrated whole. The 3-Circle model provides an integrated view of these three principles and allows a team to quickly understand the current nature of competitive advantage in their markets. The 10-step process for 3-Circle growth strategy development is summarized in Figure 9.6 with an additional brief description of each step.

One of us recently gave a talk to Notre Dame alumni in San Francisco. At the reception following the seminar, a conversation with new, incoming MBA students in attendance was joined by Ryan Else, an entrepreneur who had recently graduated from the Notre Dame executive MBA (EMBA) program. Ryan told the tale of his most recent company, Corte, LLC, a manufacturer and marketer of environmentally friendly chemical products. The company had developed a product called Corte-Clean, which is a nontoxic, chlorine-free agent for cleaning composite decking

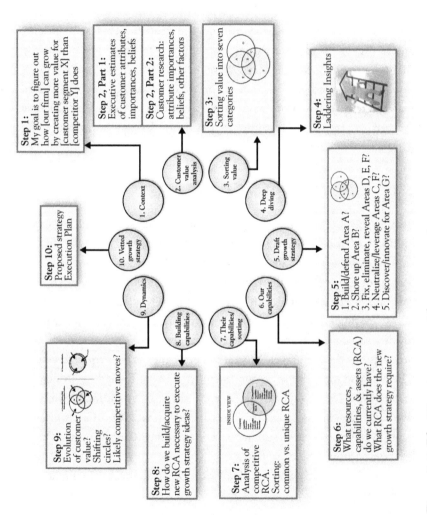

Figure 9.6. The 10-step process with summary points.

material commonly used for backyard decks. Ryan had developed the competitive positioning strategy for Corte-Clean in a 3-Circle growth strategy project in his EMBA marketing core course. With composite decking increasing from 2% to 20% of all decks, yet with the cleaning-solution category dominated by existing players, the company needed a solid positioning strategy to leverage that growth. The 3-Circle analysis revealed that Corte-Clean could be most powerfully positioned against competitors PSC, Behr and Olympic, with a focus on the absence of harsh chemicals (eco-friendliness) as the core of Area A, supported by ease of use and shelf life. It turns out these values all mattered a great deal to customers. Taking an even deeper look at customer buying behavior, though, Ryan's analysis revealed that the company's Internet site could become an important sales tool after discovering the importance that customers place on subscription sales plan and worry-free regular ordering called AutoShip. These were key insights on which Corte LLC developed strategy for penetrating key retail partners. The company went from about 100 stores in 2007 to over 3,800 stores in 2010. Sales of Corte-Clean more than doubled between 2007 and 2009, and sales in the first 4 months of 2010 have exceeded all of 2009 by 44%. The product is now distributed domestically through Lowe's, ACE Hardware, True Value, and 84 Lumber, and has stretched, through its website and through international distribution, to Germany, France, Spain, England, Australia, the UAE, and Scandinavia.

While Ryan generously attributes the success of his new venture to his 3-Circle project, in fact, the 3-Circle model cannot take credit. That success was a function of the Corte team's determined market insight, development of an innovative product that delivered on important customer values, a solid website, and dogged persistence in getting distribution. However, the case study does illustrate effective application of the principles that lay a foundation for effective competitive strategy with which we began this book:

- Create important value for customers
- Be different from (better than) the competition
- Build and leverage your capabilities with an eye toward the desired customer value

In sum, Ryan's company has now crafted a unique competitive position in its market, and that position is built upon the firm foundation of a truly, substantively different product that customers (and, subsequently, retailers) highly value. The primary credit that the 3-Circle model can claim is in helping to keep all eyes focused on the value sought by customers, the desired competitive position, and building the capabilities that allow the team to deliver on that position honestly. As with many of the case study successes we have explored in which the 3-Circle model has been applied, in the end, Ryan's product *matters* more to customers than do competitive products. That is something worth growing.

Notes

Chapter 1

1. Katz (2008, July 8). Also, Salter (1998, October 3) notes that proposition 103 highly regulated the insurance industry and cost Progressive $60 million in refunds.

2. Jaworski and Kohli (1990, December 7); MacMillan and Selden (2006); Sheth et al. (2000); Kim and Mauborgne (1997, January–February).

3. Porter (1980, 1985).

4. Wernerfelt (1984); Barney (1991); Porter (1996).

5. Day and Nedungadi (1994, April).

6. Slater and Narver (2000); Narver and Slater (1990); Kirca et al. (2005).

7. Hambrick (1982); Cohen and Levinthal (1990); Oxenfeldt and Moore (1978).

8. Davis et al. (1986).

9. See Hoch (1988); Urbany et al. (1991); Parasuraman et al. (1985); Moorman (1998).

10. In the past year, 155 executive MBA students who have participated in 3-Circle projects have been surveyed about the insights they obtained from customer research required as part of the project. Sixty-three percent found insights from customers to be "very surprising," while over three-fourths (76%) reported the research "suggested customer needs they hadn't thought of before." Of greater interest, though, is that 88% agreed that the customer insights "led to some obvious conclusions about what we should do."

11. Peters et al. (2005).

12. Sauer (2007, June 1).

13. Areas D, E, and F in Figure 1.3 are all labeled "disequity/potential equity" because they represent attributes currently providing no value to customers but, in fact, may provide the *potential* to provide value.

Chapter 2

1. Investopedia, a Forbes digital company. Rangan and Bowman (1992) were among the earliest to explicitly discuss commoditization as signaled by "increasing competition, availability of 'me-too' products, the customer's reluctance to

pay for features and services accompanying the product, and pressure on prices and margins in general."

2. Kordupleski (2003), chap. 1.

3. The Perdue chicken example presented here is a standard case for explaining the basics of customer value, and is sourced from Gale (1994).

4. Day (1994, October).

5. We thank Viva Bartkus for suggesting this term.

6. Higgins (2008, June 1); Haberkorn (2008, May 28).

7. This dimension of the model is informed specifically by the works of Day (1994, October), Barney (1991), and Kumar (2004).

8. IBISWorld (2010).

9. Tomlinson (2000).

10. Wilkie (1994).

11. Joseph (2009, May 27).

12. Arnst (2003, April 8).

13. As an example, see the curriculum developed by Tom Reynolds and team for teaching children a framework for decision making. See the website http://lifegoals.net/ and Warner (2004).

Chapter 3

1. Gelb (2003).

2. Sarvary and Elberse (2006).

3. You will also be able to ask some people why they have chosen B over A in the past, for many people likely have patronized both service stations.

4. These segments are based upon Mobil's classic market segmentation research; see Sullivan (1995).

5. Winer (2002).

6. Note that there will also be new fixed costs involved in the marketing of the new product (e.g., a separate advertising budget and distribution costs). As long as these fixed costs are less than the incremental contribution of $40, segmentation and differentiation is a more profitable strategy.

Chapter 4

1. Larreche (2008a, 2008b). Consumer firms are the focus here because they were the largest category of firms in Larreche's study.

2. This notion is standard to many conceptualizations in the disciplines of marketing and in the trade literature on measuring customer value and satisfaction. See Zeithaml (1988); Kordupleski (2003); and Gale (1994).

3. To see a basic accounting of the types of choice rules that consumers may use in decision making, see Bettman (1979); Wilkie (1994).

4. Parry (2002).

5. The six lessons described here are based upon a variety of sources, each source reflecting an important contribution to the literature on strategy. These include Peter Dickson's (1992) work on competitive rationality and market dynamics, Theodore Levitt's (1980) work on differentiation and associated dynamics, Chan Kim and Renee Mauborgne's (1997, January–February) work on value innovation, and Tom Reynolds's work on laddering and values (Reynolds and Gutman 1988).

6. Miskell (2005, January 17).

7. Wirthwein (2008), p. xvi.

8. Byron (2007, July 16).

9. Thaler (1985); Urbany et al. (1988); Compeau et al. (2002).

10. Hui and Zhou (1996).

11. We use the term "customers" (as opposed to "consumers") to provide a general reference that would cover both business-to-consumer and business-to-business markets. It is important to note, however, that the term is *not* meant to refer only to current customers. Generally speaking, there is value in sampling current customers, potential customers who have never tried your offering, and especially customers who have tried your offering but whose business you have lost.

12. Although, as we know, growth projects can be defined in almost any context (e.g., internal company projects, personal projects, projects for charities), for simplicity in our description of the process in these chapters, we refer to the company unit of analysis as "the firm" and the two alternative choices as "our brand" and the "competitive brand."

13. As described in Fishbein and Ajzen (1975), among the classic models, importance has been captured in different ways. Fishbein's (1963) original model held that beliefs about objects are weighted by "evaluations" of the attributes, that is, both the belief that an airplane was noisy or roomy and then the positive or negative evaluations of whether noisiness or roominess were good or bad. Edwards's (1954) classic model of subjective expected utility defined attributes more as outcomes. The theory suggested that an individual's attitude was a function of the probability that choosing that alternative would lead to a given outcome, and the *value or utility* the individual placed on the outcome. A third framework, instrumentality value, held that a person's evaluation of an object on each attribute would be weighted by the value importance, defined as the degree of satisfaction or dissatisfaction the person would experience if he or she obtained that object and its outcomes.

14. Oliver (1977, 1980). See also Oliver (1997).

15. Kordupleski (2003), pp. xvii–xviii.

16. There are a variety of research approaches that are used for understanding deeper customer motivations for purchase and consumption behaviors that consumers may have a difficult time articulating. For excellent discussions of projective research techniques, see Wilkie (1994); Churchill (1999); and Madison (2005). Gerry Zaltman's well-known work in the use of metaphor in studying consumer motivations is the topic of a recent book Zaltman and Zaltman (2008). For insight into *laddering*, see Reynolds and Gutman (1988; footnote 5); Reynolds (2006); and Wansink (2003).

17. Schroder (2009, October 23), p. 28.

Chapter 5

1. "Tang Gets a Second Rocket Ride" (2010).

2. Kano (1995); Kuo (2004). See also Gale (1994) and the previously cited works of Kim and Mauborgne (1997, 2005) and Levitt (1980).

3. Kano (1995).

4. The analysis is based on media accounts, including "iPad vs. Kindle" (2010), "Apple's iPad" (2010), and *Espinoza* (2010, March 1).

5. The phrases "points of parity" and (later) "points of difference" come from the work of Keller (2008).

6. "Most Important Factor" (2010, January).

7. Ali (2010).

8. Ali (2010).

9. Javier (2010).

10. Ali (2010).

11. Ali (2010).

12. This term comes from a client who described this area as a "swampy mess," in that it could represent value that had grown up organically but was no longer of value to customers.

13. Jaroslovsky (2009, December 7).

14. Better Business Bureau (2004, May 4).

15. There are a variety of research methods that exist for exploring customers' motives for purchase that they may find difficult to articulate in simple direct questioning. For excellent discussions of projective research techniques, see Wilkie (1994) and Churchill (1999). For ethnography, see Madison (2005). Gerry Zaltman's well-known work in the use of metaphor in studying consumer motivations is the topic of a recent book by Zaltman and Zaltman (2008).

16. Mohl (2006, July 10).

17. For additional discussion of this paper, see the opening of chap. 2 of Rangan and Bowman (1992).

18. Richard D'Aveni (2007) of Dartmouth College has recently examined several cases that make use of objective measures of price and product features.

Chapter 6

1. Hogan (1957).
2. Kim and Mauborgne (2005).
3. Porter (1985).
4. Solsman and Ziobro (2010, May 4); Bryson (2010).
5. "10 Things Microsoft Did" (2010, March 4).
6. Ohnsman and Cha (2009, December 28); Saad and Hill (2010, February 25).
7. http://en.wikipedia.org/wiki/Moore's_law
8. Fredrix (2010).
9. Mohammed (2010, March 2).
10. Carrns (2007, March).
11. Dhalla and Yuspeh (1976).
12. Binkley (2009, November 6); Sains (2004, April 26).
13. Rangen and Bowman (1992).
14. Bachman (2009, October 14); Associated Press (2010, May 3).
15. Byron (2007, September 4).
16. Young (2010, April 20); *Business Wire* (2010, May).
17. In our view, some of the most helpful frameworks can be found in Eric von Hippel's (1988) work on innovation by studying lead users; Rao and Steckel's (1998) insightful chapter on studying unmet customer needs; Christensen et al.'s (2007) framework on customer "jobs"; and MacMillan and McGrath's (1998) study of the customer's consumption chain.
18. Brown (2010, January 28).
19. Young (2010, April 20); *Business Wire* (2010, May).

Chapter 7

1. http://www.youtube.com/watch?v=nkuOuxRD1Bc
2. Christensen (1997).
3. Hamel and Heene (1994) provide a nice description of the variety of depictions of the internal mechanisms of the firm.
4. Rigsby and Greco (2005).
5. Wernerfelt (1984).
6. Dubois (2009); Boyatzis (1982).
7. Dubois and Rothwell (2000).
8. Dubois (2009).
9. *Iowa Alumni Review*, 45.
10. Porter (1980).
11. Barney (1991).
12. Hamel and Heene (1994).

13. Stiglitz and Mathewson (1986).

14. Barney (1991).

15. Salter (1998, October 31).

16. Salter (1998, October 31).

17. Salter (1998, October 31).

18. Salter (1998, October 31).

Chapter 8

1. Moon (2010).

2. Dickson (1992, 1997).

3. A number of scholars have examined value migration and industry change, including D'Aveni (1994), Mintzberg (1994), and Miller and Friesen (1982).

4. This case is based upon media accounts and personal discussions with physicians and other health care professionals. Key resources include Winslow (1998), Tully (2004, May 31), Gurel (2006, July 24), Johannes (2004, September 1), Burton (2004), and Kamp (2010, February 10).

5. The challenges that people have in estimating the likely reactions of others to their own actions have been discussed widely. One paper on competitive decision making found that only a minority of managers considered *competitors' future reactions* in either describing past decisions or making future decisions. Across two studies—one examining actual managerial decisions and a second examining decision making in a simulated business gain—they were *most* likely to discuss current internal factors (e.g., sales/revenue goals, costs, capacity constraints), which are known and can be controlled with much greater certainty (see Montgomery et al. 2005). For discussion of the evidence and explanations of a low incidence of considering competitor reactions, see Urbany and Montgomery (1998) and Moore and Urbany (1994).

6. Prahalad and Ramaswamy (2000).

7. There are a variety of excellent case studies in Wipperfurth (2005). For example, the author describes the original music-sharing website as the prototype of a brand takeover by users. The founder developed a means of sharing music among users online with no intent of financial gain. Users stood to gain only in that the more people who participated, the more music that was available. A community spirit emerged because users were on the front end of helping build the idea from its inception and in having a joint sense of control—and a sense of rebellion.

8. Von Hippel (1988).

9. Coyne and Horn (2009).

10. Harreld et al. (2007).

11. Gerstner (2002), p. 123.

12. Chandler (1990).

13. Gersnter (2002).

14. Harreld et al. (2007).

Chapter 9

1. The branding and category information is disguised for confidentiality, but the example is built around an actual application of the 3-Circle model.

2. For the exception to this, see Burke (2006).

3. More information cannot be provided without divulging proprietary information.

References

10 things Microsoft did to make Windows 7 a success. (2010, March 4). *eWeek*. Retrieved from http://www.eweek.com/c/a/Enterprise-Applications/10-Things -Microsoft-Did-to-Make-Windows-7-a-Success-613232/

Ali, S. (2010, January 28). IPad vs. Kindle. who wins? Wall Street Journal, Blogs: Technology News and Insights. Retrieved from http://blogs.wsj.com/ digits/2010/01/28/ipad-vs-kindle-who-wins/

Apple's iPad: Pros, cons, and toss-ups. (2010, January 27). *ConsumerReports .org*. Retrieved from http://blogs.consumerreports.org/electronics/2010/01/ apple-ipad-tablet-iphone-ipod-touch-review-pros-cons-entertainment-work -price-data-itunes.html

Arnst, C. (2003, April 8). Count calories, not carbs. *BusinessWeek*. Retrieved from http://www.businessweek.com/technology/content/apr2003/tc2003048 _5670_tc024.htm

Bachman, J. (2009, October 14). Southwest says passengers flee bag fees. *BusinessWeek*.

Barney, J. (1991). Firm resources and sustained competitive advantage. *Journal of Management, 27*(1), 99–120.

Berg, J., Matthews, J., O'Hare, C. (2007). Measuring brand health to improve top-line growth. *MIT Sloan Management Review, 49* (Fall) 61–68.

Berry, L., & Seltman, K. (2008). Management lessons from Mayo clinic. New York, NY: McGraw-Hill.

Better Business Bureau. (2004, May 4). Better Business Bureau analysis of cell phone complaints reveals root causes of customer dissatisfaction. Retrieved from http://www.bbb.org/us/article/better-business-bureau-analysis-of-cell-phone -complaints-reveals-root-causes-of-customer-dissatisfaction-470

Bettman, J. R. (1979). *Information processing theory of consumer choice*. Reading, MA: Addison-Wesley.

Beverage industry analysis and statistics. (2010, July). IBISWorld, p. 24.

Binkley, C. (2009, November 6). Famous fashion label: The sequel: Chanel had nothing on Vionnet; can a legend be resurrected? *Wall Street Journal*.

Boyatzis, R. (1982). *The competent manager: A model for effective performance*. New York, NY: John Wiley.

Brown, D. (2010, January 28). Apple iPad—5 ways Amazon Kindle can still win. *BNET*. Retrieved from http://www.bnet.com/blog/media/apple-ipad -5-ways-amazon-kindle-can-still-win/6162

Burke, S. J. (2008). Market success requirements, capability requirements, and positioning: A tool for identification and linking. *The Business Review, Cambridge, 11*, 26–31.

Burton, T. M. (2004, September). Approval of neck stent spurs debate over stroke prevention. *Wall Street Journal*, p. B1.

Byron E. (2007, July 16). P&G's global target. *Wall Street Journal*, p. A1.

Byron, E. (2007, September 4). How P&G led also-ran to sweet smell of success. *Wall Street Journal*, p. B2.

Carrns, A. (2007, March). Branching out—Banks court a new client: The low-income earner. *Wall Street Journal*, p. A1.

Chandler, A. (1990). *Scale and scope*. Cambridge, MA: Belknap Press.

Christensen, C. (1997). *The innovator's dilemma: When new technologies cause great firms to fail*. Boston, MA: Harvard Business Press.

Christensen, C., Anthony, S. D., Berstell, G., & Nitterhouse, D. (2007). Finding the right job for your product. *MIT Sloan Management Review, 48* (Spring), 38–47.

Churchill, G. A. (1999). *Marketing research* (7th ed.). Fort Worth, TX: Dryden Press.

Cohen, W. M., & Levinthal, D. A. (1990). Absorptive capacity: A new perspective on learning and innovation. In R. L. Cross & S. B. Israelit (Eds.), *Strategic learning in a knowledge economy: Individual, collective, and organizational learning process*. Woburn, MA: Butterworth-Heinemann.

Commoditization (n.d.). In *Investopedia*. Retrieved from http://www.investopedia.com/terms/c/commoditization.asp

Compeau, L., Grewal, D., & Chandrashekaran, R. (2002). Comparative price advertising: Believe it or not. *Journal of Consumer Affairs, 36*(2), 284–294.

Coyne, K. P., & Horn, J. (2009). Predicting your competitor's reaction. *Harvard Business Review*, 90–97.

Crocs, Inc. reports 2010 first quarter financial results. (2010, May 6). *Business Wire*. Retrieved from http://company.crocs.com/news-releases/ crocs-inc-reports-2010 -first-quarter-financial-results/

D'Aveni, R. (1994). *Hypercompetition*. New York, NY: Free Press.

D'Aveni, R. (2007). Mapping your competitive position. *Harvard Business Review*.

Davis, H. L., Hoch, S. J., & Easton Ragsdale, E. K. (1986). An anchoring and adjustment model of spousal predictions. *Journal of Consumer Research, 13*, 25–37.

Day, G. S. (1994). The capabilities of market-driven organizations. *Journal of Marketing, 58*, 37–52.

Day, G. S., & Nedungadi, P. (1994). Managerial representations of competitive advantage. *Journal of Marketing, 58*, 31–44.

Dhalla, N.K., & Yuspeh, S. (1976). Forget the product life cycle concept! *Harvard Business Review*, 102–111.

Dickson, P. R. (1992). Toward a general theory of competitive rationality. *Journal of Marketing, 56*(1), 69–83.

Dickson, P. R. (1997). *Marketing management.* Fort Worth, TX: Dryden Press.

Dubois, D. (2003). What are competencies and why are they important? *Career Planning and Adult Development Network.* 18(4). 7–18.

Dubois, D., & Rothwell, W. J. (2000). *The competency toolkit.* Amherst, MA: Human Resource Development Press.

Espinoza, J. (2010, March 11). E-Reading on the road: A guide. *Wall Street Journal.* Retrieved from http://online.wsj.com/article/SB100014240527487036 25304575115401843583236.html

Fishbein, M., & Ajzen, I. (1975). *Belief, attitude, intention, and behavior: An introduction to theory and research.* Reading, MA: Addison-Wesley.

Fredrix, E. (2010, April 13). AT&T rebrands self, shelves ad spat with Verizon. *Associated Press Newswires.*

Gale, B. T. (1994). *Managing customer value.* New York, NY: The Free Press.

Gelb, M. (2003). *More balls than hands: Juggling your way to success by learning to love your mistakes.* New York, NY: Prentice-Hall.

Gerstner, L. V. (2002). *Who says elephants can't dance? Inside IBM's historic turnaround.* New York, NY: HarperCollins.

Gurel, O. (2006, July 24). Drug-eluting stent market: $5 Billion turning on a dime. *MedTech Futures.* Retrieved from http://www.midwestbusiness.com/ news/ viewnews.asp?newsletterID?15086.

Haberkorn, J. (2008, May 30). Frustrated U.S. travelers forgo 41 million flights. *Washington Times*, Business section, p. 8.

Hambrick, D. C. (1982). Environmental scanning and organizational strategy. *Strategic Management Journal, 3*, 159–174.

Harreld, J. B., O'Reilly III, C. A., & Tushman, M. L. (2007). Dynamic capabilities at IBM: Driving strategy into action. *California Management Review, 49*(4) 21–43.

Higgins, M. (2008, June 1). Believe it or not, someone's listening. *The New York Times*, Practical Traveler-Customer Services section, p. 6.

Hoch, S. J. (1988). Who do we know: Predicting the interests and opinions of the American consumer. *Journal of Consumer Research, 15*, 315–324.

Hogan, B. (1957). *Five Lessons: The modern fundamentals of golf.* New York, NY: Barnes.

Hui, M. K., & Zhou, L. (1996). How does waiting duration information influence customers' reactions to waiting for services? *Journal of Applied Social Psychology, 26*(19), 1702–17.

iPad vs. Kindle vs. HP slate: A close look. (2010, January 27). *Electronista.* Retrieved from http://www.electronista.com/articles/10/01/27/apple.banking.on.color.and.apps

Jaroslovsky, R. (2009, December 7). Nook chases kindle at snail's pace. *Business-Week.* Retrieved from http://www.businessweek.com/technology/content/dec2009/tc2009127_591187.htm

Johannes, L. (2004, September 1). Boston Scientific says share of stent market has rebounded. *Wall Street Journal.*

Joseph, D. (2009, May 27). The GPS revolution: Location, location, location. *Businessweek.com.* Retrieved from http://www.businessweek.com/innovate/content/may2009/id20090526_735316.htm

Kamp, J. (2010, February 2). Boston Scientific to pay J&J $1.73B to settle stent patent disputes. *Wall Street Journal.* Retrieved from http://online.wsj.com/article/SB10001424052748704107204575039430685168478.html

Kano, N. (1995). Upsizing the organization by attractive quality creation. In G. K. Ganji (Ed.), *Total quality management, proceedings of the First World Congress*, pp. 60–72. London, England: Chapman & Hall.

Katz, A. (2008, July 8). State of the auto insurance market: An interview with Jon Swallen of TNS Media Intelligence [Web log post]. Retrieved from http://blog.compete.com/2008/07/08/auto-insurance-ad-jon-swallen-allstate-geico-progressive-state-farm/

Keller, K., Aperia, T., & Georgson, M. (2008). *Strategic brand management* (3rd ed.). New York, NY: Pearson Education Limited.

Kim, W. C., & Mauborgne, R. (2005). *Blue ocean strategy.* Boston, MA: Harvard Business School Publishing.

Kim, W. C., & Mauborgne, R. (1997). Value innovation: The strategic logic of high growth. *Harvard Business Review, 75*, 102–112.

Kirca, A. H., Jayachandran, S., & Bearden, W. O. (2005). Market orientation: A meta-analytic review and assessment of its antecedents and impact on performance. *Journal of Marketing, 69*, 24–41.

Kohli, A., & Jaworski, B. (1990). Market orientation: The construct, research propositions, and managerial implications. *Journal of Marketing, 54, 1–18.*

Kordupleski, R. (2003). *Mastering customer value management.* Randolph, NJ: Customer Value Management.

Kumar, B. (2004). *Marketing as strategy.* Boston, MA: Harvard Business School Publishing.

Kuo, Y.-F. (2004). Integrating Kano's model into web-community service quality. *Total Quality Management, 15*, 925–939.

Larreche, J. C. (2008a). *The momentum effect: How to ignite exceptional growth.* Upper Saddle River, NJ: Wharton School Publishing.

Larreche, J. C. (2008b). Momentum strategy for efficient growth: When the sumo meets the surfer. *International Commerce Review, 8* (Autumn), 23–34.

Levitt, T. (1980). Marketing success through differentiation—of anything. *Harvard Business Review*, 83–91.

MacMillan, I., & McGrath, R. G. (1997). Discovering new points of differentiation. *Harvard Business Review*.

Madison, D. S. (2005). *Critical ethnography*. Thousand Oaks, CA: Sage.

Miller, D., & Friesen, P. H. (1982). Innovation in conservative and entrepreneurial firms: Two models of strategic momentum. *Strategic Management Journal, 3*(1), 1–25.

Mintzberg, H. (1994). The rise and fall of strategic planning. *Harvard Business Review*. January–February. 107–114.

Miskell, P. (2005, January 17). How Crest made business history. *Harvard Business School Working Knowledge*. Retrieved from http://hbswk.hbs.edu/archive/4574.html

Mohammed, R. (2010, March 2). A new pricing plan to lure "dormant" customers. *BusinessWeek*. Retrieved from http://www.businessweek.com/smallbiz/content/mar2010/sb2010032_742820.htm?link_posit

Mohl, B. (2006, July 10). Meet the corporate research department. *Boston Globe*. Retrieved from http://www.boston.com/business/articles/2006/07/10/meet_the_corporate_research_department/?page=2.

Montgomery, D. B., Moore, M., & and Urbany, J. E. (2005). Reasoning about competitive reactions: Evidence from executives. *Marketing Science, 24* (Winter), 138–149.

Moon, Y. (2010). *Different: Escaping the competitive herd*. New York, NY: Crown Business.

Moore, M., & Urbany, J. E. (1994). Blinders, fuzzy lenses, and the wrong shoes: Pitfalls in competitive conjecture. *Marketing Letters, 5*(3), 247–258.

Moore's Law. Wikipedia. Retrieved from http://en.wikipedia.org/wiki/Moore%27s_law.

Moorman, C. (1998). Market-level effects of information: Competitive responses and consumer dynamics. *Journal of Marketing Research, 35*, 82–98.

Most important factors in buying a car. (2010, January). *Consumer Reports*.

Narver, J. C., & Slater, S. F. (1990). The effect of a market orientation on business profitability. *Journal of Marketing*, 20–35.

Ohnsman, A., & Cha, S. (2009, December 28). Restyling Hyundai for the luxury market. *BusinessWeek*.

Oliver, R. L. (1977). Effect of expectation and disconfirmation on postexposure product evaluations: An alternative interpretation. *Journal of Applied Psychology, 62*, 480–486.

Oliver, R. L. (1980). A cognitive model of the antecedents and consequences of satisfaction decisions. *Journal of Marketing Research, 17*, 460–469.

Oliver, R. L. (1997). *Satisfaction: A behavioral perspective on the consumer.* New York, NY: McGraw-Hill.

Oxenfeldt, A. R., & Moore, W. L. (1978). Customer or competitor: Which guideline for marketing? *Management Review, 67*, 43–48.

Parasuraman, A., Zeithaml, V., & Berry, L. (1985). A conceptual model of service quality and its implications for future research. *Journal of Marketing, 49*, 41–50.

Parry, M. (2002). *Strategic marketing management: A means-end approach.* New York, NY: McGraw-Hill.

Peters, C., Thom, J., McIntyre, E., Winters, M., Teschke, K., & Davies, H. (2005). *Noise and hearing loss in musicians.* Retrieved from http://www.musicmotion .com/content/mim/pdfs/hearinglossmusicians.pdf

Porter, M. (1980). *Competitive strategy: Techniques for analyzing industries and competitors.* New York, NY: Free Press.

Porter, M. (1985). *Competitive advantage: Creating and sustaining superior performance.* New York, NY: Free Press.

Porter, M. E. (1996). What is strategy? *Harvard Business Review.*

Prahalad, C. K., & Ramaswamy, V. (2000). Co-opting customer competence. *Harvard Business Review, 78*, 79–87.

Rangan, V. K., & Bowman, G. T. (1992). Beating the commodity magnet. *Industrial Marketing Management, 21*, 215–224.

Rigsby, J. and Greco, G. (2003). *Mastering strategy: Insights from the world's greatest leaders and thinkers.* New York, NY: McGraw-Hill.

Rao, V. R., & Steckel, J. H. (1998). *Analysis for strategic marketing.* Reading, MA: Addison-Wesley.

Reynolds, T. J. (2006). Methodological and strategy development implications of decision segmentation. *Journal of Advertising Research*, 445–461.

Reynolds, T. J., and Gutman, J. (1988). Laddering theory, method, analysis and interpretation. *Journal of Advertising Research, 28*(1), 11–31.

Saad, O., & Hill, S. (2010, February 25). Credit Suisse identifies 27 great brands of tomorrow. *The Street.* Retrieved from http://www.thestreet.com/ story/10689574/credit-suisse-identifies-27-great-brands-of-tomorrow.html

Sains, A. (2004, April 26). Marimekko is looking groovy again. *BusinessWeek.*

Salter, C. (1998, October 31). Progressive makes big claims. *Fast Company, 19.* Retrieved from http://www.fastcompany.com/magazine/19/progressive.html

Sarvary, M., & Elberse, A. (2006). Market segmentation, target market selection, and positioning, pp. 85–97. In A. Silk (Ed.), *What is Marketing?* Boston, MA: Harvard Business School Press.

Sauer, P. J. (2007, June 1). More volume! *Inc.* Retrieved from http://www.inc .com/magazine/20070601/features-more-volume.html

Schroder, M. (2009, October 23). Getting to the bottom of things. *Quirk's marketing research review*, 26–29.

Selden, L. & MacMillan, I. C. (2006). Manage customer-centric innovation—systematically. *Harvard Business Review.*

Sheth, J., Sisodia, R. S., & Sharma, A. (2000). The antecedents and consequences of customer-centric marketing. *Journal of the Academy of Marketing Science, 28*(1).

Slater, S. F., & Narver, J. C. (2000). The positive effect of a market orientation on business profitability: A balanced replication. *Journal of Business Research, 48,* 69–73.

Solsman, J. E., & Ziobro, P. (2010, May 4). New recipe lifts Domino's profit. *Wall Street Journal.*

Stanford, D. (2010, April 26). Tang gets a second rocket ride. *Bloomberg Businessweek,* 32–34.

Stiglitz, J. E., & Mathewson, G. F. (1986). *New developments in the analysis of market structure.* Cambridge, MA: MIT Press.

Sullivan, A. (1995, January 30). Mobil bets drivers pick cappuccino over low prices. *Wall Street Journal,* p. B1.

Thaler, R. (1985). Mental accounting and consumer choice. *Marketing Science, 4,* 199–214.

Tomlinson, C. (2000). Reconcilable differences? Standards-based teaching and differentiation. *Educational Leadership, 58*(1).

Tully, S. (2004, May 31). Blood feud. *Fortune.*

Urbany, J. E., Bearden, W. O., & Weilbaker, D. C. (1988). The effect of plausible and exaggerated reference prices on consumer perceptions and price search. *Journal of Consumer Research, 15,* 95–110.

Urbany, J. E., Dickson, P. R., and Key, R. (1991). Actual and perceived consumer vigilance in the retail grocery industry. *Marketing Letters, 2*(1), 15–25.

Urbany, J. E. & Montgomery, D. B. (1998). Rational strategic reasoning: An unnatural act? *Marketing Letters, 9,* 285–299.

U.S. airlines last year made $7.8 billion in fees. (2010, May 3). *Associated Press.*

Von Hippel, E. (1988). *The sources of innovation.* New York, NY: Oxford University Press.

Wansink, B. (2003). Using laddering to understand and leverage a brand's equity. *Qualitative Market Research, 6*(2), 111–118.

Warner, F. (2004). Ethics? Ask a first grader. *Fast Company, 83.*

Wernerfelt, B. (1984). A resource-based view of the firm *Strategic Management Journal, 5,* 171–180.

Wilkie, W. L. (1994). *Consumer behavior* (3rd ed.). New York, NY: John Wiley.

Winer, R. (2004). *Marketing management.* Upper Saddle River, NJ: Prentice-Hall.

Winslow, R. (1998, September 18). Missing a beat: How a breakthrough quickly broke down for Johnson & Johnson. *Wall Street Journal,* p. A1+.

Wipperfurth, A. (2005). *Brand hijack.* London: Penguin Books.

Wirthwein, C. (2008). *Brand busters: 7 common mistakes marketers make.* Ithaca, NY: Paramount Market Publishing.

Young, B. (2010, April 20). Brand repositioning: How to save an "uncool" product. *Pacesetter Global.* Retrieved from http://www.pacesetterglobal .com/2010/04/20/brand-repositioning-how-to-save-an-uncool-product/

Zaltman, G., & Zaltman, L. (2008). *Marketing metaphoria: What deep metaphors reveal about the minds of consumers.* Boston, MA: Harvard Business School Press.

Zeithaml, V. A. (1988). Consumer perceptions of price, quality, and value: A means-ends model and synthesis of evidence. *Journal of Marketing, 52,* 2–22.

Index

Page numbers followed by an "f" or a "t" refer to a figure or a table on that page.

Announcing the Business Expert Press Digital Library

Concise E-books Business Students Need for Classroom and Research

This book can also be purchased in an e-book collection by your library as

- a one-time purchase,
- that is owned forever,
- allows for simultaneous readers,
- has no restrictions on printing, and
- can be downloaded as PDFs from within the library community.

Our digital library collections are a great solution to beat the rising cost of textbooks. e-books can be loaded into their course management systems or onto student's e-book readers.

The BUSINESS EXPERT PRESS digital libraries are very affordable, with no obligation to buy in future years.

For more information, please visit WWW.BUSINESSEXPERT.COM/LIBRARIES. To set up a trial in the United States, please contact SHERI ALLEN at *sheri.allen@globalepress.com*; for all other regions, contact NICOLE LEE at **NICOLE.LEE@IGROUPNET.COM**.

OTHER TITLES IN OUR STRATEGIC MANAGEMENT COLLECTION
Series Editor: Mason Carpenter

CPSIA information can be obtained
at www.ICGtesting.com
Printed in the USA
FFHW010858101218
49771084-54282FF